Life in Poems

LIFE IN POEMS

Deborah Ferneyhough-Sweet

Life in Poems
Deborah Ferneyhough-Sweet

Published by Greyhound Self-Publishing 2020
Malvern, Worcestershire, United Kingdom.

Printed and bound by Aspect Design
89 Newtown Road, Malvern, Worcs. WR14 1PD
United Kingdom
Tel: 01684 561567
E-mail: allan@aspect-design.net
Website: www.aspect-design.net

Cover Design Copyright © 2020 Aspect Design
Original photograph Copyright © 2020 Sandra Pugh
ISBN 978-1-909219-71-7

This Poetry Collection is dedicated
to my Father.

Donald George Sweet

A Tewkesbarian Man:

August 1931 ~ January 2002

ABOUT THE AUTHOR

Deborah Ferneyhough-Sweet was born in Tewkesbury, Gloucestershire on December 26th 1958 to Donald and Barbara Sweet. Her father was the owner of the well respected firm B Sweet & Sons Undertakers.

Deborah is married to Charles Ferneyhough, and they have three grown up children, and three grandchildren.

Deborah is the published author of *Forest Diaries*, 2013. She writes short stories and poetry and is an exhibiting artist.

~~~

Earth's poetry calls his pen soft, like love's thought.

Ivor Gurney

~ WORDS ~

By Edward Thomas

Out of us all
That make rhymes,
Will you choose
Sometimes ~
As the winds use
A crack in the wall
Or a drain,
Their joy or their pain
To whistle through ~
Choose me,
You English words?

I know you:
You are as light as dreams,
Tough as oak,
Precious as gold,
As poppies and corn,
Or an old cloak;
Sweet as our birds
To the ear,
As the burnet rose
In the heat
Of Midsummer...

Make me content
With some sweetness
From Wales
Whose nightingales
Have no wings, ~
From Wiltshire and Kent
And Herefordshire,
And the villages there, ~
From the names, and the things
No less.
Let me sometimes dance
With you,
Or climb
Or stand perchance
In ecstasy,
Fixed and free
In a rhyme,
As poets do.

A Nurturer of Nature in Word,
Silent in thought, but the thoughts are a storm,
and a Multitude that will move mountains

Deborah Dawn Ferneyhough-Sweet

POEMS

BEYOND THE WALL

The last embers of the night, bed down
Grey grate flickers of its lights soft sounds
And I am dreamin', through the floorboards
The young woman is me, and feels a history
Known, but unknown.

I latch up the door, creeping the small steps
Into the known, and crosses time unknown
I hide and see beyond the wall, I watch him
Into our room, where we both live, known.

Ablaze those embers now, beyond the wall
I look at his face, bright aglow, from all fires
He dreams with me, into the grey grate of war.
In his armour he stands ready there to depart
Far from the homeland that he knows
Into the face of a foe, and all wretched wires
We, unknown, but known, I unknown.

My grey grate of war, looks back at you
And caught in thought, unknown you stare,
Into the orange light, as bright as flares,
And I know, your unknown, histories tells
For England's youth, their terror and fates
Of the trench, and the mud, and the shells
When we look to war, in our grey grate.

1980

This is a Dream of mine, when I was 23 years old, and I was
living in a cottage at number 7, Well Alley, Tewkesbury that had
been built in 1854. The cottage was under renovation by us, as

we were working and living in the cottage at the same time. One night I had this dream that was so real to me, and it has stayed with me all my life.

The open fire's embers had died down for the night, as I slept. Then in my dream I had cause to go down stairs, as I could see the fire alight, and beaming up towards the floorboards above. I peeked down through the floorboard cracks to the fire down below, and felt that someone was in my house. As I took to my stairs to creep quietly, I had to quickly cross the doorway, and peek through this hole in the wall, as I did not want to be seen. There in the next room stood a soldier in first world war uniform, he was as young as me. His face was aglow as he stared into the fire that lit the whole room orange. I watched him in great detail, hoping he would not notice me. I will never forget his face, he looked so sad to leave, with wonderment to whither he would return, I could still pick him out in a crowd to this day ... It always felt to me that history had crossed between us, and that I had dreamed into his past. Perhaps he once lived in my cottage and was brought up here, and left his presence behind. The memory of this in later years, struck up a poem in me, which I dedicate to the unknown soldier beyond the wall.

BLOODLINE

These ancient roots vein through the land
And seeds of old plague rich her soils
Seasons upon seasons, down centuries' time.
Flint to the rocks these, "O men of Earth"
Generations by, remembers not your toils
Where wolf and bear 'both' hungered blind
They were your kill, your fill, your warmth
Took over their caves, and fully occupied,
Made fire, ate animal, and clothes from skins
Long from a time, when river sank at north,
When 'men of earth' lived upon Laurasia.

2010, Forest Doward Fort

BORN CONNECTION

It said it all, a picture imagined
That crumpled paper in the bin,
It said it all, with arms embraced
It said it all, 'love' eyes connected
'Will you still love me tomorrow?'
Mom and the world, she sings.

Mom says my big girl (looks up)
Amy says your big girl (don't worry)
Mom says my little girl (mother's love)
Amy says your little girl (child's love)
It's just the way it is, I can take it.

The little bird on the world's wire
Shone, this star in darkness bright
With her songs, that set hearts on fire
Sparkles still into our starry night.

Now absence brings, no more she sings
God's time here, is only borrowed,
Exchanged it all, for feathered wings
Amy, 'we will still love you tomorrow'.

2011

This poem is dedicated to the singer, Amy Winehouse. I was aware of her untimely passing in 2011. She was young, beautiful, and talented, and at the height of her fame.

Amy to me, was every woman's daughter, and everyone's sister. For me, this poem was prompted by the image in a newspaper, I found in a bin, whilst at my work in Gloucester.

Amy and her mother, were in an embrace, that the camera had caught. Daughter was tall, mother was small, and they were looking into each other's eyes.

My heartstrings told me of my own daughters, that for mothers and fathers whatever choices our children make, you will always feel their pain, and more, and you will always love them.

"And yes, we will still love them tomorrow."

CALLUM

From Ledbury those green hills and blazing sun
In this English garden of roses and peonies,
Came message to me, you were in the world.
First breath, the day your life had begun
When I was later in my years.
My child, my son, his son, and birthed from me
As if there could ever be another,
And the joy of that gave me my tears
For what had come from my son's mother,
He is your father, I am your grandmother.

There I stood within Green England's bliss
Was birthed to this land, old poplar trees
Where within the sun and glistened in turn
Quivered warm winds, their silver leaves,
And there were you in all my mind
Amidst them shining like the stars,
Callum you were they, in all the summer,
Of summers, that you now are.
And your face, in the flesh from silver leaves
I will endeavour to see you very soon,
Wanting to place, upon cherub cheek,
A grandmother's loving tender kiss
In this summer of summers,
Our boy is born the Sixth of June.

The sixth of June 2006 my first grandson Callum was born to my son and his wife Emily, their first child. I was to be a grandmother for the first time, and we were waiting for the birth of Callum to arrive. I was working in Ledbury for a lady in this rich English country garden, full of Englishness and of old well established variety flowers. The message came as I stood alone amidst these English blooms, and looking afar to the hills and woods of Ledbury, poplar trees in their finest glory came to me. Hence the poem of 'Callum' he were they.

Written Sixth June 2006

CARRIAGES OF HEAVEN

Lifted eyes upon sight, mine a child's delight
Wonderment to the ore, of these multitudes
Whose terrain, is raw, seeking the light,
Buried over in the slidden slatted weight
High amongst split crags of silver slate.

Nature did'st give you a garden of Eden
Touched mighty, by the breath of God,
Yellow and purples, millions upon us, where,
Wales' wailing winds, sway their colours in turn
As we marvel and travel in carriages steaming
Through mountains, with waters streaming.
Here his eyes look down in fairness and care
Unclenching his hand, to falling sunbeams
That ride fast with us, across the rugged land.

On high above, dances the gliding mists
The soaring buzzards about their peaks
Then comes forth tumbling its heights
As treasure from heaven's broken purse,
Pearly streams falling helpless, and seek,
With speed, hunted out is its every channel
Drowned and buried its force, and hence
Against the proudest mountain rock.

Below; the lagoons of dark beauty drinks
In deeply at its mouth, and resting place
To a still mirror of heaven looking back,
To the image of, God's pure face.

August 2009 North Wales, Llyn Cwellyn

CHOOSE ME

Will you choose me?
A forest poet, those woodland words?
Melt my heart, I choose you;
Wide eyed, never ending her skies
Buzzards' high cruises, their cries heard
You chose me ... true Wales blue.

All of you that is fair and lovely
Wales first birth of England. Laurasia;
From there her mothered mountains
Sits nurtured full, her bosomed purses,
First milks, pure heaven rains given spills
Tumbles the wild rocks, creviced fountains
Falling willing to the vein her river fills.

He my rock commands, the sweet waters
That carried me vesselled, safely through
Within the beating heart of Wales,
HE CHOSE ME ... I CHOSE YOU
Will you choose me??
My Salvation Home ... True Wales Blue.

All that is lovely Wales, like God true ... The giver and his creative handy work of earth ... God is here my Salvation home ... 2011

COASTAL PROSE

Morning has Broken

I watched from my bed, the coming dawn upon the sea woods, and the light rose up from the sea, and worshipped the heavens, and I knew all was well with me.

The gulls in great multitude upon those shelved cliffs, came to their calls, all beckoning the day,

and the rooks returned from the night to claim back the sea woods, another day begins.

Goodbyes from my Window

Where the chimneys' woodfires mist the airs, and gulls preen the day away in new hours, upon the small stacks,

in the bright morning light, that in turn reflects off the calm and soothing tide ... And the robin's shrill came to me for all his attentions, piercing the invisible airs. Then I with you walked away to the sea brambles, where from the lookout a dry ship waits, waiting for the coming hour, sits in patience to the horizon, upon the glassy sea.

Michael John Walton

Man of the stars, moon and sun, old and full of years, your wisdom comes from the core of the earth. Gentle care and thoughts is yours, it has no end, and it will live forever, like the ebb and flow of a new tide, your words cleanse me. The heart is a precious thing to possess, and you gave it freely with all blessings. The almighty came from your lips, in the embossed book of life, which I held dearly within my soul.

Beer in Dorset, 2013

COME TAKE MY HAND

I could live within the soul of the woods, happily
She is my true being complete, a soul consumed
By all her birds wing and songs they sing in turns,
Gives woodland flowers' scents to the hum of bees
In all of her heart, born is beautiful forest seasons
Upon her maiden paths, greets the bowing trees,
To find him always here; in poetry; he gave to you
God permitted me to stay, and he gives no reasons
Returns me back to the woods, with many and few;
With the thoughts and voice of poems and words
He says 'Come take my hand' dearest Wales true.

Then I stood alone in the forest after the rains

Came soft forest rains bathing her beauty
In earthy mists those heavy clouds fountains
Soon stopped in silence with the sun then,
Falling in fresh airs, sunbeams like diamonds
Glinting from towered heights through glades
Refresh the forest floor in tiny trickled streams
Beneath my feet, and with all gladness to be,
Still with you where I can fill my forest dreams.

Softly the voice of God rustles on the winds
'Come hold my hand', dost thee fearest not
For I the breath of God is true upon this land,
I the life's soul in rock and mighty mountains
You are all mine, 'come now take my hand'.

The cycle path, Forest of Dean, Sept 2013
"Poem to coming home"

25

COMETH

Low lights of winter the afternoon's chills
Shadows warmth to ride the green vales
Sink hues horizons between bosom hills,
Of the fairest of lands is greenest wales;
High in a blue sky sits the moon white
Reflected back from the fiery planet
Big whole white moon sits into the night,
And the blackbird sings away his last call
Into the tall yellow firs, edges my picture.

Over my shoulder by the hedge and verge
The woollies of Wales' nose, close the land,
And the brook babbles in tune, to my mind
Deep it has creviced, deep it has purged
Far from its birth, long gone is its woods.

Shading eyes with the palm of my hand
Robin bids me farewell, singing close by,
The long winter night is now what I find
Whilst the chill of the stars twinkle silver,
Feeds my bones to the close of the day
White beams the moon, whole in my sky.

2014, Monmouth: by Bond and Bunjup Woods

LANDS REALM

Wittered, withering, and wandering
Hard to keep it in the fold
Through the centuries a squandering
To a pound, to a penny in a purse,
Let it die fingered, in estates sold
For a blessin', or for worse,
Into laps born, and titles, yet another lord.

Quarried and rooted, alone upon the hill
Built hard, from earth's Cotswold stone,
Through ages and through glass, here I view
Many hands to a king, given from the throne
Coscombe rides hard across the rural land
Where God's heaven is weathered wild blue,
Mighty Malverns, commands the counties
Within this green England, Englands so true.

Nov/Dec 2011, I worked at Coscombe Manor.

LANDS REALM REVISITED

The sheep on the side, the way on Cotswold,
I travel the familiar path winding on through,
Up o're grid and crafted wet mossed walls
By many a man's toils in years hands of old,
And to greet me refreshed to eye and mind
The angelic nodding snowdrops, earliest.

And a thousand thoughts and speech unfold,
Into this land, a conquered place I did hear,
Their voices before me, long into the winds
I come again in flesh with chances; my soul,
And my spirit rises again and back hath found,
To sky, earth, my counties' bloods in crowns.

Arrived soon upon the hill cutting in at all winds,
That swept o're the bosom across the flat lands
Up through into me towards Coscombe Manor.
Yellow Cotswold golden in seventeenth grandeur
For I am with you once more, with my chances
Looking out to my love, finest green England.

2014

I have come back to embrace to embrace you once more with all
my chances "praise God I was saved"

CORN BY THE RIVER

The laney track by old locks way
There field and coppice, lures traveller in,
To a canopy and dark overhang
Knitted lacy brackens all astray,
Where tiny birds flit, and blackbird sings.

The darkened route towards the end
Beacons, backforth, a white sunlight,
To a dusty road, with twisty bends
In company, banks of emerald grass,
Sways with the coming autumn breeze
Whilst river flickers, like tinkling glass
Tall silverleaf rustles, the poplar trees.

Beyond the wires, and an aged gate
Lay golden plains, like the desert sands,
That bowed in wait, for the steely sickle
To winters cause, arrives man's hands.

Haw berries rich, a great crimson sea
Bustles fair winds in turn, all places,
When once was white, all in youth's bloom
Pure as fallen snow, those bridal laces.

By tow path, old iron clanks us by a pass
O're that small tranquil river, its divide
And bistort floats pretty pink in mass
By the boat tied old, at river's side.
While into depths, fish up, do they look
At flitty wings, and touchy toes dancing,
Teases gentle, upon their world's surface
Jumps out to sunlights, fast advancing.

Now one turns away, to a path good worn
Where summer left behind, a garden of eden,
Of mayweed, woundwort, and toadflax born
Rainbowed heavens colour, to wings abeating.
And by the river there stood the tallest corns
Like a well dressed army out on parade
Regimented fell straight, to perfect forms,
These eight foot troops, take a look inside,
Wears feathers in caps, with golden braids.

2012, Old Tewkesbury Lock.

DANCING QUEEN

There she was, my little dancing queen
Slender and long, beautiful and strong
The daintiest child, you had ever seen.
Ivory silks ribboned, the towers of her legs
Her pink net frillies, bobbed twisty her waist,
On her toes she spins, lifted pink on her pins
Spray sticky slick back, hair young and black,
Those dark pools, of dreams, her eyes did stare.

There she was my little dancing queen
Dancing to song, beautiful and strong
The prettiest child, you had ever seen,
Prancing butterflies soft and bathing tune
To the hard keys play, in the dusty school room.

Now the years have gone by like falling snows
When the girls and the crowds, gathered all of a throng
And their parts on the stage, echoes age, in a show
Full of laughter, and claps, mothers tears, children's song.
But still she is Jezica, mommy's special dancing queen,
The most beautiful woman, you had ever seen.

1992

Jezica, my first Daughter, started dance school, in the early 1990s with the Janet Marshall Dance Studio, at the Abbey School Rooms, from the age of four years old. Ballet she loved, and was born for it. She was in many shows in Cheltenham. Two shows were "The Snow Queen" and "The Silver Curlew" and she did dance for nine years.

FATHER

Summer 1964

My childhood friend remember me
When past those days fields were gold,
And there I ran free in careless bounds
A thousand miles through desert stubble,
And there skies fell, to a bowing dusk
I remembered you, that ambered place,
Where father walked across your plains
His path struck scarlet, as I looked back
Content and happiness was in his heart,
Is etched into my mind, his happy face
My thoughts where he, will never be old.

2010

This early memory is of my father Don Sweet. We were walking the fields of the 'Ham' in Tewkesbury, and upon our return home, the burning sun was going down, bowing away scarlet, ending the hot summer day.

The red glow from the sun befell its last shafts of light upon the fields, where harvest had been gathered. The stubbles of grass remained, beaming up golden against the fading light.

I looked back at father, as he carried my sister on his shoulders, looking blissfully happy, where his image from out of the dusk was surrounded by a crimson light, upon the path he walked.

I was young, but this memory of my father imprints my mind of colour light and love.

FIELDS OF FORTHAMPTON

The river flows below and I climb
Breathless I, caught to the fields
On the hill of late ambered lights,
Amidst the harvest dust and yields
I am standing with Ancient Britain
Being part of the histories' time.

Yonder, rises transparent flitty wings
The thousands, in their times of gold,
From earth, ambers shadows of beam
Falling from the sky in its heat of blood
Within my fiery planet's creation of old,
Echoes bird songs last, the night brings.

The brown hares, how they loved you
Our Ancient Britain, there we are born
Amidst the landscape of our rich soils,

Came saplings sharing seed and thorn
Through ages they rise with strength
Upon seasons from the ancient length.

In my time; I am here the participant
Dreaming by my hand and in words,
Stand the giants' white ghosts forms
Clings to the earth broken in death
Lived out, but dead they still serve,
They; the wandered white elephants.

———
2013

FIRST HARVEST

I remember you still in your forties' fashion
Sat on a small stool in that sunny garden,
With tall blooming stocks in pink and white
About you, as your gnarled hands kept busy
Bidding me to come over and shell with you,
Grandfather's peas tended, he had grown
Picked and waiting earth, in an old tin bowl.

That still Sunday morning in the shadows
Sat in the aromas of mint and lemon balm
And we two, both with old tatty pinafores
And colanders on our laps, you smile,
Knees to knees, "Oh how I so loved you"
No mother grander than a grandmother.

The fat podded peas filled my small hand
Bulging, fit to burst with great surprises and I,
Popped those earthy firm sweet juicy jackets
Uniformed like soldiers stood all in a row and;
Grandmother's eyes down were busy popping
I slyly popped them disguised into my mouth,
But she had seen, and with smirky smiles said,
Your mam! with me won't be very pleased
Spoiling your dinner with grandfather's peas.

1964 at 17, Oldbury House, Tewkesbury
dedicated to my grandparents Doris & George Sweet.

FLOWERS FOR SHOWERS

A young life had left us, come to an end,
Amidst the sunshine and cool showers
Upon the springtime of April's soft tears
And early morn when the blackbird sings,
Lovely the road, neighbour's blackthorn;
He left his friends behind in the early hour
"Mark" in all the joys, a child's smile brings.

Cry not for me dear friends, my heart is warm
For I have gone with you to be young forever,
And even though I know your hearts are torn
I watch you all and smile through, that is true;
Now exchange your tears in my April showers,
For happiness and love and all summer flowers.

2014

In Memory of Mark Walker a dear friend to all, who gave and left laughter and sunshine in the hearts of all who loved and knew him. "Come little children unto me".

GRAVES END

To the millions, birthed giants of long ago
To the trillions, rolls tiny with ebb and flow
Made carved, where sea treasures do return,
Awaited their fate and the crushing tides.
Those little dainties painted, wrapped in gold
Worn by ancient slopes, bleed endless stream.

The sea is still claiming, century by century
Dragging away into its great mouth by entry
Its prehistoric neighbour, ever ever closer,
Making through a passage, to the land.
And the sea, receding back from its call
Left behind, pockets of warm rock pools
That with mermaids' hair swirls, waiting still,
Of pinks, greens, silver, with pearly shells.

Gripped razors sharp black, to coraled rock,
The silvery grains shimmer in morning's sun
Like the plains of a desert, glints granite.
Yonder by sea, the dark hanger of a cliff
Hollow, a shallow cave of silver sand
Lured me there, a lagoon of jade waters,
Made ready for love, all of me, I am yours,
Wanten of you, waiting, waiting, waiting.

Charlestown, Cornwall, 10th Nov 2009

HOME FOR CHRISTMAS

Christmas 2006 Callum when you were a babe,
Upon the dark night and hidden crisp moon
My first, my babe in arms, you came to stay.
That night the stars twinkled, and jack frost
Sparkled, marooned, and marpled its sting;
Against the thin sticks vacant of silver leaves
That once danced about your summer born,
Amidst the blazing heats, the golden sheaves.

Here now in the silences of winter you sleep
Cherubim winged by my side, cradled to keep,
Still; but awake piercing the dark with your life
Wanten for love, rustles your summer breeze.
And I; sharp as any mother, but grandmother,
Pricks up her ears in the mind body and spirit
Reaches into your innocent, instinctive embrace.
And I; took you to my bed, holding you close
Reading your mind, into mine, like a good book,
So the words read, from your cherubim smiles,
In the small hours, lights beam from your face.

And I; put my nose to yours 'yes' we two had met
We had met here once before, many moons ago
"Us";
Blue eye pierces, blue eye back into each other,
Mine; to the old world, yours; to the new world,
And the old sayings go with us that we two are,
The voice and spirit of our many grandmothers
Connecting forever growing and falling from,
Those towering sounds from the blousy trees
Popular; the poplar; rustling; glistening; song,
'You Callum' forever your lights of silver leaves.

By your Grandmother, Deborah Ferneyhough-Sweet, 2006

I AM THE VOICE

I am the voice, the small voice
A voice calling in the wilderness,
I am the rain's, coursing the veins
I am the soul of her soils
Where once my foot light had trod,
Crushing not the sleeping bulbs
Of life, coming into the flowering day.

My cells have caressed barks of many
By mind; hands, breasts, and my face,
I am in, and have worshipped all them.
I am the voice, seduced by the ghosts
And I gave all myself to her wantonly,
With purpose, redeemed, once again.
I am the voice in those secret places
With all her winged and hoofed children,
Honoured, am I to be their mouthpiece.

I am the voice in her language found
We speak; and I will sing my praises
For she is the diamond in a king's crown;
Her beauty magnifies a thousand queens.
I am the voice of rocks, woods and water,
Sank a crevice, where life had brought her
I have travelled through on her like blood
Where crawls out the creatures of man
From his small beginnings, I am the voice,
I woman, I mother, I ... a surrogate in love.

———
2014
I am the Earth's mouthpiece and voice of the forest.
Written from Sister Rock over the river Wye towards Staunton.

I REMEMBER TULIPS

I remember tulips, 'oh how I remember tulips'
Those red clasped petals, the tears of blood,
Waiting waiting to fall because love has died.

I remember tulips ... how I remember tulips
Those pink clasped petals, tears of absence,
Waiting waiting to fall because love has gone.

Tulips, I see tulips, watching and waiting for ...
The beautiful death that seems forever lasting,
And those petals, soon they are falling, falling.
Helpless ... down to the reality of hard earths
From where they had once came, new born,
Falling through light airs, I watch love dying.

1987/2008

IN MIST & BEAM OF TIME

From afar in places upon rock and hill fort
Little wisps of wavering white mists appear
Arising from, within the soul of the forest
As if the ghosts of abodes still here exist.
From their woodfires to cook and keep warm
Foresters living, working, by drovers' paths,
With beasts and their own kind works the land
As the foreigners from other places do pass.

"They had left their ancestors behind them
And I leave they; my ancestors behind me,
You will leave me; your ancestor behind you".

For ghostly mists arise in forms from the woods
Is the fine elements of God's worldly creation
Tuned by his mind and hand is what I do see,
From the universe casts a fiery planets beam
Down upon the earths of the forest's floor
where many moons of man, within its seams,
Lie in earth no more, release soon to awake
Rise up! away through the open forest doors
Into earthy airs and past the old occupants,
Are your familiar friends, once their residents.

Rise up! to the heavens, meet with God's warm touch,
Through beam their ghosts escape the spindled trees
Into the skies, past the universe, thrown from heaven,
Where first we came to be, swimming pools of liquids
Mineraled, Microscopic, Atomed, into creatured seas,
He pulls us back out of the earth, where we last fell
When life gave us purpose, to breathe and groan,
The agonies of his promise, into the earth and forests
From the cradles to the graves, in mists and beam.

2013

From the beginning of time, when life was so small and naked to a human eye, that was not possible for us to know about ourselves, but we, in full view from the creator God. As time evolved our natural ends with the beasts of the earth that lived with us and still do, we fall back to the earth, decomposing and composing within the layers of seams in the earth's formations of time making it what it is. We all contribute and distribute our matters into the natural world, and have our turn in that, but hence where we came from, the heavens home and God's hand created, through the universe to earth.

Through mist and beam: The beam from whatever earths age and time, is the fiery planet settled in gravity from the universe that makes us live. Throwing its great heat upon us, reaching into the soul of the earth, by opening its doors in warmth drawing all matter to itself, back up to the skies beyond its place, in the mists that become mingled a blend from the scientifics of its being.

The mists developed then become a transporter, taking us back to him. Whilst God is a great scientist, this is what I relate to in living and knowing about ourselves, and understanding God in his elements. This is what I see in mist and beam, it is the other side of the coin of life.

JEWEL CREST

A dawning day, is a good part morning
Through the narrow lanes, they begin anew
Where fields feed families, from their labours
Are babes not here, and came, are but few.

Stands white and grey, the old church Pendock
Like the lonesome horse, vacant without friend,
While mountains neighboured, blue and faithful
Commands sky and land, dominant without end.

From the glass box, looks far to ridge and furrow
Multitudes rich dandies, a sea of golden waves,
Whilst old oaks giants, grateful to keep their places
The thrush sings bold, through the close of the day.

In the spring of April 2011 we worked at a cottage in Pendock. The cottage had a room adjoined that was all glass, so all the fields could be seen at three angles. I sat down on my break and wrote this poem here. An old Norman church could be seen in the distance, against the sun, by a wood. The golden tides of dandelions beaconed away from us into a few fields to the church. The edges of the wood were finely laced with blackthorn. The pheasants were on fine form fighting, one male pheasant flew straight into this glass box I was working in, I was convinced that it had broken its neck. On further investigation the bird wobbled off as if drunk off through the field's edge. And the thrush did sing plentiful, from 6am until our 5pm.

IN MY SKY

I look up into my blue sky
Just underneath my cherry tree,
And into the brightest sunlight beams
There you are, flying free, we are three,
Flitting transparent wings, as they dance
Above within, the last sun is a chance.

Belonging fawny wings up upon high
Souring the thermals' invisible streams,
This time is ours, in my mind, you are mine
In all my hearts fading, I have yet to find,
More of earth, wanting more of my dreams
When I am with you, in my blue sky.

June 2013

In the moments of resting at home in the garden under my cherry tree, and looking up at the sky at the buzzards, and life in the insect world within the warm balmy sunshine, I was grateful to still be here after the shock of being in hospital from heart failure, and having tests at Bristol, which was not long after my first book Forest Diaries was published. I did not know what my future held for me, and all my plans of enjoying the fruits of my labour and enjoying an audience for my book were very misty. The plans before it happened, to cover the bigger picture of my Forest Maps on foot, for another publication was on hold, if ever …

KYMIN

A winding road, old and familiar there,
Where grandmother's root ties her Kymin
Things best kept tidy then ehh! she says,
As tidy as the spring nests in May ...
Umm I will keep that in mind rhyming?
Speaks the mind, away and pennin'.

Then upon Kymin approach, flew overhead
Struggled at low heights, those fawny wings,
Where on its tail in tow, flew the black mob
All a croaking in throat, they hoped to win,
In a locked on chase, to loot her booty prize
While forever hungry, were waiting in the nest,
The buzzard babes, crying out upon Kymin's rise.

The talon's grip, she could hold no more
And fast that rabbit was released and fell,
Deep down into spring, the lacy mays
See now, where did the heavy host fall?
Invisible, to the bottomless pit of the day ...
Lost within the white snows of forest floor.

'Look now' upon dark hill and shaded overhang
A deer had fell, and lay soft upon the green slope,
His gun is bowed silent, at the wooded edge
Where at last the hunter's barrel did explode
Into her hide so small, and yet still warm
Like her blood ... it cools with the blasting lead,
In pastures a forest, she lies sleek and fawn.

2010

I did not expect to see so much going on about me in the car, as
we travelled the road through past Kymin, towards Monmouth,
where it seemed this place and some family secrets were ... so in
Kymin with the mind, my pen starts a pennin.

EASTNOR FIELDS

These days of summer are well in pursuit
Weaved within June's longest dusty lanes,
And hedgerows married, to all bird songs
Pulls away into fields and farthest beyond,
At the great gate, redder soils bled more
Sparkles with the sun's heat, and my pain.

And yet the coming harvest is still young
Regimented swaths the multitudes' tides,
Of many a mauve bell bloom, silent rung
When bumble's quivered wings all a hum,
My heart is still here, fears my tears I hide
In the heat of June under God's red sun.

Thank you God that I am still here to live
To feel your earth, and yet strive to give
My soul to others, in my mind's words
Of earth of now, and is soon to come
God help them all, easy to understand
When I no longer walk the forest land.

I now stand in time, my time with only you,
In the midst of those bluest summer skies
Once again my own kind they come to see
Where play and teach sours piercing cries,
A distant church bell came and softly rings
And I am grateful, my ancient fawny wings.

With my tears I close my eyes and take in,
Emotions struck I cannot hide, "I so love you"
When death was black and breath was thin,
Hanging, I thought of you in my fading skies
Souring up to heaven in your fawny flights,
At last God gave me chance, he gave me life.

Then:

My love alone he walks the Eastnor fields
Away from me to soothe his empty pains
But there is a life we have not lived yet,
And only God knows, I have no regrets
About plans he has, and what is truly best
Those thoughts for us, thoughts for yields.

In sunlight's low and lastly blinding scorch
Upon the hill the fiery planet golden casts,
In shadows, like kisses of the sea's sands
That burns so bright, God's burning torch,
Beyond, beasts move slow within its earth
God give me hope another day, make it last,
And I will see again a morrow, another birth.

Eastnor potato fields in the month of June 2013
My hope in life after escape in death.

LET'S GO DOWN TO THE OLD RIVER

Autumn calls, undarkened the lane appears
Where we walk the green wet fields beyond,
Through berries red, down by a water's edge
Let us walk, as we both talk, holding hands.
You soothe my mind when comes my tears,
To better years, than the ones left behind.

There we walk nearby looking to its decline
The old river owns her ghosts with a bend
Where sunken souls uplift their last place
Into the mud, where is no flow, just ends.

Unknown the heron stands on one in hope
In canopy of withies down by the river bed,
He, tall and sleek, lank with his grey coat
About stagnant waters, the grey silent edge
Darts the dipper hurries fast foraging nearby.

Look out to the old river, vacant from its work
I could fill her soul again, with all of my tears,
Through purple clovers, reeds, soft grasses
Within the rivers of faith and God's good earth.

Yonder the inclines led us to an untrodden path
You offered me up and through with your hand,
And my heart had lost its way from light a little
Through hawthorns, hips, sloes and brambles,
Into the canopy of earth we two came together
Chasing the adults from us as we scrambled.

Where, hidden nearby in ages past dark arches
Further still from the old river's stagnant moat,
Stands in the centuries time of many a man's life
A giant of magnificence, stood the 'mighty oak';
Where earth and the waters come close to meet
The incoming night that chills my skin to shiver,
As we walk golden sunsets by vessel and rope
Take my hand, 'Let's go down to the old river'.

Upperload, by the old river, Sept 2013

MAD ENGLISH MAN IN THE MIDDAY SUN

Old salted face, wild of the west
Imagines she came forth from a sea
Crawled out, and became what is she,
Happily burns out, in a midday sun
And you hangs yer rusty layers above
Building the stages of years in millions
The Cornwall skies commands blue
Watchin', seems forever, over you.

The fiery planet surely reaches in
With its burning midday flames
Soaking up all the attention
As our flesh runs, runs to chase.
Was I, upon your ancient sands?
Bared all to the old sun gods
Exposed, and ready for embrace,
And here my youth returns
So light in dreams, no shame.

Flickers many mirrors upon the tides
Like rushin' in wide, to meet my love
Holds him in years to silver, set in stone,
And here we still are together, older grown,
Always being with Charles, you, by my side.

Charlestown, Cornwall, 26th Sept 2009

MAISY

Familiar was I the place by iron track
Where river Wye flows through beneath,
There came a grand chestnut lady mare
A trotting briskly down from lone lane
With a prettily coloured braided mane.
She stood silent when mistress took a drink
Dark pools for eyes they looked to mine
And I wondered of me what did you think,
As mistress talked of you and that was fine
About your agonies of those pains and twist,
And how the young chestnut lady is still alive.

I stroked your nose and soon could not resist
A further look into your mirrored eyes, and talk,
About lady's time, now to that I could relate
When sometimes rest is so behind the gate,
Our futures held set to be just a little hazy
When we all escaped deaths clenched fist,
That chestnut lady mare her name is Maisy
Soon bounds up the lane with her mistress.

2012/2013
The Boat Inn at Penallt

53

MAN OF THE WOODS

There was in the forest
Along the Doward's way,
Through shady trees of leafy glades,
We met a man of woods called Mike
Friendly was he, with his forest mates
Cus strangers was we, by quarries gate;
The man of woods, he welcomed us in
Told stories of his, he trusted us true
Cus there we loved, all the same thing
Friendship was made, as laughter grew.

There was in the forest
Along the Doward's way,
Through shady trees, of leafy glades,
Our friend was there, now rides a bike
All on his own down by quarries gate;
Here came a stranger, but not a mate
He's not trusted true, not welcomed in
The stranger be, he clapped his hands
Cus he with us, loved not the same thing,
Friendships not made, this volunteer clan.

There was once in the forest
Along the Doward's way,
Through shady trees of leafy glades,
The man of woods, he is not there
He absent be, down by quarries gate;
Cus the stranger now is on the rocks
She is not there, no babes, no mate
Unwelcomed foe, untrust they flew,
Once here a gem, within the forest fare
Were stories gold, and friendship true
We love the same thing, the same as you
With friends and birds, came all to share.

This is a poem to a man called Mike, who we met in the forest when we first started to walk Doward in 2008. He was a lovely forest man, and a real Man of Woods. He was dedicated to his past time, in the forest with the deer, and the birds of prey. He spent many hours watching them, and watching out for them. He cared deeply about the forest, and was full of stories. He accepted us, and trusted us, and let us use his equipment to view the birds of prey, in the forest, down Doward's way. Mike he is the 'Man of Woods' and he really made me laugh when he told me of a time he had been in the forest waiting for hours, in a proper hide out, to see these deer. As he thought he would have a drink from a can in his bag, he pulled the ring on the can when suddenly realising that the deer were very near his hide out it was too late as the deer heard the 'psst noise' which he could not muffle, and the deer ran away.

MINIONS AND MOOR

Tufted rufted twisted the surrounds
Many sparse prickled old gorses
Lichen bent trees keeping the divides
That ill winds take turn in their courses,
Draft to shiver, damp bodies aquivers
Right to the bones through fattest hides.

Mossed and holed the mounds dipping
As all waters come from any quarters
Streaming through landscape dripping,
Ever on in past ages then and still now
Fertile and barren both mind gripping
To men of men, horse, bull, and cow.

Rich forms carve in mineraled springs
Sticking hard to the clods of the moor,
On man and beast in flesh and bones
Carried the seed of them on ever more
Work and breed, with perishing groans.

The moor's winding road so far from coast
Echoes thundering hooves so wild and free,
Proudest is the herd that leads the way
Through thicket and tree, many his family,
With manes and tails the cascading veils
And thickest coats that warmth will boast.

And:

The bounding rabbit and stretching hare
Is the watching tower of buzzard's glare,
Where mouse and mole is in his sights
Gains taloned grip from swooping flights.

Folklore:

The lean black cat prowls the moor
Is seen in the sleekest blackest form,
Such beauty in its eyes, to kill more
With hunger in its belly and on breath,
Fear reigns, as mighty is the capability
Its pangs will it fill, brings on easy death.

Take a good look it is frozen by the gate
Where eyes did meet, posed in a stance,
Majestic black, strong, primed and lean
Slopes low fast by, won't take a chance,
And stories do tell that folk have seen
The black beast lies drowned its fate,
Now dragged up from the bottom silts
Of its watery grave from Siblyback Lake.

Written at Lyncot cottage, Common Moor, Minions Cornwall ... 2012

This is a true story told to me by my sister-in-law Maryanne who
lives at Minions on Bodmin Moor, the person in question she
knows well has seen this beast at the gate with horror. 'A chance

meeting'. There has been evidence of the presence of this cat or cats, as on the moors horses wild and domestic are kept in the part fields. Lacymay, my sister's horse, with the other horses kept here on the moors have been found to be disturbed in their behaviour showing fear and disturbances from the night and early mornings. It is a bleak place and could be any century.

MY SUNDAY GARDEN

At times there is nothing to enchant
Until I awake with a mind so new,
I walk within my sunday garden
And gentle in silence take a pew.
Early birdsongs begins a morning
Fresh upon my deary flowers, the dew,
Just as the sun was ambered rising
I entered the world's hour of dawning.

The bumbles I heard on many flowers
And it gleed my heart for they are mine,
God's creatures busy these few hours
Amidst the sun, escapes fine showers.

My lavenders blue dilly dilly
My lavenders green silly silly
They will be true all on time,
They are all mine willingly
Where wings purpled do dine.

Scarlet dangles the bean blossoms
Aquivering with wings all glows rosy,
Whilst dainty the spearmint and chives
Forms lilac blooms of a perfect posy.
The shock spray of old pink shamrock
Embraces the lawns of clover white,
Whilst the old rose climbs up the wall
To the years of sixty, against the clock.

And the children's towering sunflowers
Taller than giants, grows ever reliant,
With their brightest yellowed powers
And their heavy plated heads all round,

Drip those stripy seeds afalling plenty
Back down gently, rested to fertile ground.

The six foot tall mustard umbrellas of dill
Draped heavy dewed or feathered ferns,
Kept wings dancing the tempting nectars
Tunes to the fine morning airs that they fill,
In tiny blooms, bees are the great selectors,
Afrenzied about those dizzy heights in turns.

2012

MY TIME WITH YOU

I have to write to you tonight
By the dusk into my candlelight,
Where all sunsets are part of June
And birdsongs are falling from the noon.

We climb evermore into those wooded hills
Blasting through the winding dusty road,
As one we go, I with you and you with me
As if still young, 'aye' nothing's changed.

Born apart, we should have been twins
It was our love God gave to both of us,
Within the past, 'parted' within the sins
We ride hard the road in summer winds
To my blue mountains, into warm rush.

Where in our youth we came here before
With fine chances we did not die too soon,
Returned again we two, this familiar place
On the steep dusty road into another age
With fine chances I did not die and stayed.

We two as one on two wheels where is fun
The canopy of woods taken darken our way,
Through bends and turns and speed we go
Back to blue mountains, back into the sun
Back to our youth together, now we will stay.

To the British Camp at Malvern, 2014
We have returned to the life we know.
We have returned to who we are,
That no death can destroy.

SR 500 yamaha 1980
SR 500 yamaha 1980/2014

NO MORE

The Bird within me was dying
But the Bird was dead at my feet,
Although my mortal being was fading
It was my master of the skies, and not yet me,
Within the forest's slumber and winter shading
Slumped to soft grasses the old tombs to rest
His peace came under darkness of the yew tree.

No more will his fawny wings become splayed
To soar those heady heights within sweet airs,
No more on the wing is he the eye in the skies
Above forest and river and fields where life plays;
No more his calls to me is heard in his eerie cries
Lying silent his form, I stare into death at my feet
His heart, no more, where mine is fading to beat.

And I left death amidst the rivered snowdrop beds
Where the whitewashed church vacant still stood,
I left the river, Brockweir bridge, forest, her woods,
I left the long road out, sooner to return as dust;
But the whispers of the forest held me closer
Unknown they spoke … 'Tis not your time to go'
I did return and much wiser, still I see her river flows,
I walk her woods and waters, seeing her pretty fare
To my senses, her scents, her spirit, and in all I trust;
Will be mine forever. No more into his death I stare.

2013

Before it all went wrong Brockweir was my last visit to the
forest. I had been chasing the Wye Invader dutch barge up
the river before her departure from Brockweir to Bristol for

drydock. In this last week before it all went wrong I came back on the Sunday to see if the barge had moved with the right water depth conditions. It had gone early in the morning and I had missed her departure from Brockweir bridge. I proceeded to walk over the bridge and into the village to visit the old church and graveyard. The river had been up and had left behind a lot of straw dragged from the fields yonder. The straw and debris of trees and wood had banked up over the graveyard, knitting a fine weave over the strong white old stock snowdrops, which did not deter them rising afresh to the season appointed. In this Brockweir graveyard were the resting places of oldest residents that died of anything along with most of their children. My foot suddenly came to the body of a fine male buzzard that had died at the foot of an old yew tree, and I stared into its life of no more. At this time I was unaware how ill I was and because I have a closeness to buzzards I felt the life further drain out of me, literally. The buzzard was untouched and beautiful even in death. Suddenly within our midst came a lady from nowhere into the grave yard, she looked about the small humble headstones and spoke to us to say those people are my ancestors. She continued to say that it was the first time she had visited the village of Brockweir from across country but knew of her family here in the 1800s. When she looked down she asked what the date was, we told her ... "Oh", she said, "that's strange, this is the very day this lady, my ancestor, died many years ago" ... and on that small headstone was the same date as today ... We thought it strange too then she continued to say that upon that hill, pointing to an old barn, my ancestor, the husband of this lady buried here, built a farm so the children had a better way of life. But she stressed that the date on her ancestor's headstone was unknown to her until now, on the very day of her visit.

As we later left Brockweir that day, the following week I was ill with undiagnosed heart failure, and I survived by a miracle.

PADSTOW

We chase the sun again, returns its fiery surprise
All in its newness, like summer had just begun
Upon us all embraced, a second summer birth
Then another day arrived new, with mist and burn
To a land's bright divide, with an early mornin' rise,
And the golden sands where, the sea takes its turn
Is the rushing of the tides, down by estuaries flow
A place linked us familiar, a place called Padstow.

The days serve us so idle, upon the salty winds
Fast the 'fury vessel' sprays, cutting Cornish tides
Through surfy waves, there her mammals dwells,
And play with us do they, in dark emerald swells
Where babes attach grey, close by mommies' sides
Flipping up the waters, quick by their diving fins.

Old Enodoc is ageless, in the distance golden lay
So far now and too late, for me to sit and relate
My respects to a poet, this poet could not keep,
Cus old pains were a damned, to reach your way
As I muse in far centuries, falls in sunken sands
There a poet's words stays, where a poet sleeps.

Padstow late September 2011. A sudden comeback of a new summer heat wave, made everyone chase the sun. When leaves were yellow and falling with the fruits of the year, we chased a second chance in Padstow.

In this week we boarded a speed boat called 'sea fury' to see the dolphins. This was not guaranteed, but the dolphins did appear, and with their babes, swimming fast alongside us at distance. With the great swells of the tide, I was elated to find my camera had caught one mother with her babe, by her side grey and glistening.

I wanted to visit the grave of John Betjeman, but could not risk the distance, because I had a torn knee cartilage, and was awaiting surgery. We stayed at the 'Slipway' B&B in Padstow, and the lady here told us that John Betjeman often used to come into the harbour to sit and talk to people.

PERCEPTIONS OF STUPIDNESS

Oh wait a minute! whilst I die
The fading spirit of my own heart
The faint beat, "Oh wait a minute"
Whilst I die slowly to the clock,
All worry and tears about my bed
I knowing soon, I have to depart.
Oh wait a minute! whilst my words
Keel over and die away with me.

I paid you very well, and yet!
You repaid me with a dud brain
As if I would not find you out,
No apologies, as if my pedigree
From your perceptions of little me
Are dud brained to all my stupidness?
Oh wait a minute! Whilst I die some more
To all men's inadequacy and idleness
And all your bloody lofty negligence.

In silence, add insults to my injuries
That you have not done your best,
When I wrote, and worked to promote
My own words, to what I love the most,
And your silent tongue is full of lies
When the world could have known me sooner,
Oh wait a minute! whilst I take your mistakes
And your dud brained perceptions of …
my STUPIDNESS.

2013
Disappointments can be dear.

RACE ME

For a feast, the cloak sprawls its drape
Elegant and exposed, grey as the rock
Ancient and grey, as the rock you are
Where the eye in the sky, picks out fate,
Hurries by lost, from the formation flock
Flown from a cage, where abode is now far.

Safety in numbers, strayed a wing from home
'Explodes impact' in heights, mid-air tussles,
To the drivin force unexpected, unknown
Takes a drop, to an end, cuts frequency state
To a day numbered four, a year numbered eight
So a breath, and a death, parades a hooded cape.

2010

A secret location guarding technology, and survival of species of peregrine.

RED

The buzzard sits owned to this land
Through the shaft and shadows
Beam wains from wake and sleep,
Upon her belly reveals the light
Fawny winged and looks to seek
Claims the sky's elements in flight.

Alone the old man oak stands rooted
Connected; the familiar loamy red vein,
And the land that has seen him well
Within him rests, soft her secret nests,
Life for both still, in many times again
Until his time comes back to earth
Soon she will leave because he fell.

Nearby the old man clank, stands firm
Disconnected iron and steel and bolt
Came once connected and connecting,
Deep rooted and above this fair land
Cargoed carried smuts the air dissecting,
Now vacant, hear the ghost rails ride
Strewn parts the rusty wheels of steel
Lie grassed below, buried in the field.

At distance to the water's edge and land
Engineered black moulds, the grey rock,
Made industry and wages in men's hands
Stands broken in half from dynamite told,
A man fell in with her, a tumbling drop
But he lived to breathe another bad day
And lived to tell the story, when he was old.

2012

This is a poem giving insight into the once transportation of steam trains that weaved through the forest. At Redbrook walking these tracks that are now vacant from the trains, that leaves its ghosts behind in the embankments and fields down below from their great looming presence. Yes they have fell from their great heights and time has buried their working parts into a wasteland of cluttering iron and steel and wood. Dismantled bolted rails and train wheels, and even a train track turner by the bridge that used to turn the trains round in another direction, was strewn aside the tunnel it once went through.

On this cold damp day when the river Wye was high and raging, due to heavy rains in the April, underneath the viaduct, the stormy skies began to clear in pockets to allow the sun to peep through its warm ambered shafts of light upon the land. A buzzard had place here in a old gnarled oak that stood alone and not yet fell back to the land. The buzzard flew from the oak over our heads with her bronzed fawny wings taking flight to the sun in worship. As she glided in majestic form toward the sun's rays and ambered light reflected her soft belly feathers turning the buzzard to amber.

The old man oak veteran and bloodlined still to this land, and is home to the generations of buzzards born here, 'A tree of life' … The old man clank viaduct bridge was once a screech and clank of moving heavy metals with cargo and people, now silent and distant to the minds of those old men left.

Standing on the viaduct I push my head through to view the torrent of river coming through underneath me, sometimes I feel its force rumble through its structure to my body. Then I look to afar at the green land over the river Wye where stands a towering railway bridge with architectures designed and built by man's hand. This line once crossed the river from the other side, into another unknown snaking line through the forest. The grey rock it is built from looks familiar to the quarries around the forest, and the black engineer bricks built with such immaculate skill.

A lady came walking by with her dogs and we got talking to her, she said in the conversation that she could remember forty years ago that this viaduct bridge was to be dismantled by dynamite as there was no use for it, and the safety of it over the river Wye was a concern. The day came for dynamite to be applied to the bridge over the waters, and a worker was on that bridge and he was not stood far enough back or perhaps he thought he was. When the blast blew the bridge piece to smithereens, this man went down with it, but the miracle was this man survived.

RICHARD THE DOVESHEART

Richard the Tewkesbarian
Acts in theatre, plays his dords
Writes his music, sings his songs.
An entertainer, community sustainer,
Builds his own house, a business man,
In brick and raft, in willow and craft,
And in many a thing he turned his hand.

My memory of you Richard
In the old shop, the baskets you made.
The green willows soaked and twisted,
And the sticks in the air twirling a circle
As you beat down into the willows firm
With the iron block and your fingers
So sore, and hands strong and nimble,
But always with a smile to your face
And with a charm of good breeding.
With our laughter you called me Debbie,
Dear friend your company was a joy
Those years made me nine baskets
Your baskets for me ... Richard
Made with your skilled fair hands.

You were a father, a soulmate husband
But not yet a grandparent.
You were a son, brother, uncle, grandson,
A nephew, and a cousin,
A dear friend, to many a kind companion.

A carpenter, a builder, a crafter,
And the best landlord they say, and had.
A singer, a songwriter, a musician,

An actor, an entertainer, we so loved you.
You were 'Tewkesbury' and all of her
You Richard, lived rich the life of two.

And you wanted more, and could of given more
But you could not stay, but had this to say,
'We can strive to be better people'.

And as we mould ourselves to you
To be like you, in your nature true,
Your examples to love, in action.
We are empty to your presence
And empty to your absence,
But when we think of you Richard
We are full again, for what we had
And what we will be able to gain
In the joys of life, living full again.
In love you were with living
Was what you were giving.

Prepared you were for departure above
Brave, accepting, and all that was lovely,
Not religious, but acted out true in life
The honest 'christ' in all love.
Simple in living, generous in giving,
'Yourself' to everyone Richard
What a gift we had … 'we had you.'
And whilst we are still alive
Richard 'passed us his torch,'
We would be letting you down
If we pass not, love along now.

Our goodbyes in this life to you
Procession we followed streets through,
The Roses carriage, your made basket
You weaved your own last, a casket,
Carried high above down the path
Upon those shoulders, of soldiers
All in brotherhood to you so true,
Placing you upon other flowers
Amidst the dark whispering towers
Where the bird songs sang for you.

Your siblings sang in voice and chord
And she your woman told your love.
So brave, and spoke of you so well.
In the wind and fresh airs they played
Your voice sang with the dark birds
Lifted us once again, this we heard.

In our sadness your voice makes us strong
For us now past days, our hearts long
You will be helping us on, in absence
You are doing it again, in our presence,
Amidst our tears, and strength to restart
Richard you have never really left us.
Play for us forever in tune and song ...
Even though we are sad this life to part,
My dear friend to us you will always be
Ours forever, *Richard the Dovesheart*

2012
For a very dear friend and true Tewkesbarian, Richard Hughes

73

ROSIE

Rosie my dearest special friend
How you loved me that I knew,
Women of our kind did not pretend
How our laughters made us so new,
Those summer days in my mind's eye
The bestest sisters, where we all grew.

No man could part us, we were one
Under the same great glorious sun,
Rosie how I so loved, so all of you
Even when you had to go far away
Our hands joined across those plains
I, could not reach you into your days
I, now knowing of your tumoured pains.

And I, sent you a letter into your abyss
Of Jesus Christ before us, you will leave
Come sister Rosie with me I plead enlist,
Come Rosie ask him, do you believe?
The army of Jesus and everlasting life
And that letter I pray had you received.

Rosie's memories

Into the forest into those green glades
The scowls of the forest remembers
The wilderness where you once played,
Children left her with their last goodbyes
To return with her own, into the shades,
With dizzy hearts and stars in their eyes
Shared this with ours, we did with you,
Happiness in memory, all of surprise.

Deborah's words to Rosie

Sisterhood in earth and in Jesus Christ
We will meet into the spirit of the forest
Within company of the angels chorist,
Believe Rosie, it is all of God's promise
In heaven's realm, those balmy woods
Where we will walk and play once again,
And yet until then, I will live here without
My sister Rosie, my dearest happy friend.

2013
In memory of my friend, Rosie Wynter

SANDY BAY

Lead me down the regular path made
Where lilacs lady's smock, in full pastures,
Pipes the curlew's shrill, embracing song
Keeping near, her lowly nest below
Rises to flights, with us in her sights
Amidst the swaying meadow throng.

And at distance under the old oak
These starry eyed lovers lusts do play
With kisses deep, so young and new
Embraces enough to make them choke,
With hands clasped, we remember once
Our times of youth, our summer days.

Looking past to waters, and reminiscing still
We teeter gently upon the slipping edge,
Where lay remnants, from lasts risen spill
Sifted and licked away the generous banks,
When winters flood, brought the river bed.

Sweet fragranced is the fresh soapy falls
That finely disperse those pepper sprays
Giving sight to many flipped up tails
Fighting against the tide's pouring weight,
Constant is their need, that never fails.

Here comfrey rich her bells to you she rings
Of purple/pink hues, in the fading sunlight
Wades deep to our feet, whilst birds still sing,
Through brackens came, some gentle breeze
That's blessed with all of crimson blooms
Where a secret place hid, chestnut trees,
Swaying mighty to, their regiment heights.

So I save the last, and the best to come
As her robes are richly laced, and worn
Cradles the babes, in her bosoms born,
Where mothers nurse, and fathers bring
Within these jewels, young is the spring,
It is the magnificent, royal hawthorn.

2010
Sandy bay, just off the 'Ham', Tewkesbury, Gloucestershire.

SECRET

I don't know why I feel such truth within my time
And how my faith was so crushed in youth,
And how I looked to you, I wanted to believe;
That you would still see, and have need of me
In awe of the girl you loved, and gave me proof
But was prepared to leave us both behind …

Point me to the corner, making tough decisions
Out of my mind in choices, fraying at the seams
Holy at most, for one reason or the other,
Those growing cells not allowed in my dreams
Remember … I will always be your mother.

That's why I have a secret
Will you promise to keep it?
And never tell a soul,
Because it's hell trying to beat it
Drives a stake through my heart
And just swallows me whole
Dirty and dark, steely and cold.

The silver crucifix I crushed in my hand
And the white house stood upon the hill,
I awoke to … it could have been Jerusalem
In the sun's shadows where I was born,
It was Jerusalem, he had bore my secret,
My heart and mind, the years have torn
The place of thoughts still in all regret
Returned, he guided me back to his land.

_1977_
"To the Unborn"

SELF

Disruption churns aliment to eruptions
The soul of souls eternity into the seas
Spirit of the untamed in centuries,
Reaching hands loom of the famous
Story of man, it claims back and more
Unnerves the seas' dogs with purpose
Came the earth's guts, rock and shore
Upon the calms and angered surface.

Like Jonah thrown out from the boat
To be claimed within its miry turmoil,
Angered God, sent in with no hope
Swallowed up in those great rooms
Kept in forever behind death's door,
Into the bowels of the watery earths
Out cried a thousand voices of men
Deprived in knowledge were the poor.

Spewed chances, the almighty mouth
He gave upon the crest of light wave
From the east, west, north, and south
Back it will claim in the 'spirit to self';
Own will of itself, to claim or to save
Reseeded the waters from the skies
When Noah cast out the white dove,
Eternity kept them as pure wings fly
Either way back to 'self' man will stay
Untamed his spirit of the mighty seas.

2014
'God is the sea. God is the Man. God is the word. God is Almighty.'

79

SHY TO EAT

You cannot be a bird wanting to escape
And still think like a human child,
In my mind this birdie turns his nose up
At the feast of worms, cold and rubbery
Forced down the gullet beaked sharply
When the birdie would rather feast on,
Cheesecake, and yellow custard sweet
And tongue creamy, taken at its leisure,
Savouring every dollop, with pleasure.

or

You cannot be a human child
And still think like a bird,
In her mind she turns her nose up
At liver and kidneys cold and tasteless
This fuckin' gross, made to sit forever,
This affair at the table being made to sit
All afternoon, whilst she wants to be sick,
Picking over the organs from beasts and,
The cook putting on her 60s' face,
Watches me in the mirror 'enjoying it!'

She

The human child would rather eat:
Birds' seed, apples, cherries, berries
Nuts, and savouring every nibble
And the outdoor activities of flying free
Away and through the slender trees
Belonging to no one, no quibbles.

Childhood and Control in the kitchen, 1966

SONGBIRD ON A WIRE

Little songbird sat all alone
Sings sweet her melody on high
The comfy pillow by candlelight
Her place of solace, her little home,
My songbird sits upon the wire
Sings long into the starry night.

She was the last, yet not left the nest
And sang not known, to mommy's delight
I hear her songs, and her little voice,
My heart was joy, but never tired
For when she flies 'tis not my choice
Absence now brings, no more she sings,
My little songbird on a wire.

Sept 2007

My youngest daughter Daisymay, in 2007 was fourteen, her brother Charlie and sister Jezica had left home. Her best pal Kayleigh and my daughter who had been with our family since she was six, left to return back to Somerset. Daisymay was always a happy girl, and was singing to herself most of the time. Now she was alone, and the last to leave my nest.

Daisymay's room was the attic room, and one night in the dark, I stood at the bottom of her stairs listening to her singing the night away. Her tunes were sweet, like a bird in a wood. Here the seeds were sown in my heart in a poem, about my last child ... called ... Songbird on a Wire.

STALE

I sit in my bleak room
A shared room, never undisturbed
With a blank windowless view
Where I delve into my memory
When yesterdays were new.

And the pen does not write
And the key will not tap
And low moods are all black
And the purpose seems crap
Gotta get beyond this pitstop,
Cus I got bloody writers block.

2011

Feelin' sorry for myself, trapped by my knee operation and convalescing, in pain, missing the forest, can't walk it yet … My food supply's been cut off … be patient dearie …

TALK TO THE WOODS

Into the dark, stood tall and towered
Guarded by gate, a giant douglas fir,
When further into the gloried glades
There became a multitude buzzard stir,
About the paths springtime flowered
Hopped and danced the buzzard babes.

Elders were high up in those dizzy trees
Casting their wide feathered fawny wings,
Swoop low the cool earthy airs and leaves
Called down below to their buzzard babes,
Infancy danced unknown where life begins
Upon moist the forest floor, they unfazed.

Then hearing language, familiar were we
They became human, and again it was me,
To my calls they had soon answered back

My beautiful angelic and ancient breed,
Soothing my sorrows, I truly was not lost
Holding bluebells on heaven's forest track.

In my mind's eye strength again was mine
Where I took to my feet and ran the hill
Through canopied wooded glades divine,
Where bright beam shone cool the shades
Led me out away from my human fears,
I was still with company, but not alone
Soon began to feel, dread from my own.

Could I change and turn to feather
Lifting my wings up and fly forever
I am human, but can only dream
With the company I wish to keep,
In my world my will to endeavour
To stay a while with them I should.
For my golden-times are truly golden
Within the glades of Goldsmiths Wood.

————

2013
Within the old Monmouth road, in Goldsmiths Wood.

THE ACTOR

Promising, and young, 'there goes the actor'
Blossoming full of life, 'there goes the actor'
The curtains rise, as do the raging waters
Staggering in darkness on stage, here tonight.

The plunge by the oak, he passes on by
As our boy is took away on the tide,
Witness do say, of echoes call to a voice
Made his way to the grave, our actor's life,
That the raging waters wretched, did hide.

Then came dark skinned people of another land
Riding low wave, of a volunteers' band
Tewkesbury's child was lost, and found they say
Held him lifeless, by a volunteer's hand.
Frankie, sweet Frankie, he were goin' places, he said,
Walks on his way light footed, scratching his head.

In the theatre of life, all the scripts have been done
But his was short lived, in the void of a ditch
By the gate of a church, to the loss of a son,
Was 'Tewkesbury's Actor' our boy ~ Mitch.

2010

This poem is dedicated to the life of Mitchel Taylor aged 19,
who drowned in the great floods in Tewkesbury 2007.

THE APRICOT TREE

Out in the garden, was planted a seed
Where here grew a tree, taller than me,
I was your child, you lifted me with care
Up into strong arms, and love was ours;
I was so tiny as you held me closely there,
Out in the garden, with all pretty flowers
Up into the sky, I went to pick apricots,
This dear father, my mind never forgot.

Father had a garden, with an apricot tree
Where you built a home, for mother and me,
There grew a pink rose bush over the door
Where grandmother picked one for her coat,
These are the sweet memories that I adore
That rose in her coat, better than any brooch,
The rose in her coat, and the apricot tree.

Years have gone by, and I have my own
Children are mine, but no apricot tree
Into my mind there is happiness sown.
Love in my father's eyes, love all for me
Love in my heart for him, my memory,
Father and child, and 'the apricot tree'.

From memory, 1961

86

THE BEAST

A child is crying, the fruit of my loins
Left in the care, with children she played,
The child was mine, small child so fair
Spared by God, she lived that fateful day.

Damaged the beast, it disturbed, it paced
Jaws and teeth, its heavy breath,
Chased, hard and struck, with blood and pain
My child's face, her face down; its face,
locked in her lovely, chestnut crown.

She ran from hell, when God released
The beast gave chase, the beast wants more,
Quick to her heels, she ran to a darkened room,
A cornered mouse, she shut fast the door.

Aunt Maryanne gave her, a Christmas gift
Of silky braid, to tie her chestnut mane
Now slobbered made, torn, ripped and pink,
Swirls thick and crimson in a sink.

Came back my father's face, in a dream
Not happy he dressed in jumpered brown
To warn with anger, in a vision
For all the lies, and coming division,
Cus, grandchild blood cried up to him,
Remains now with family, a wretched sin.

2001

Division, and cruelty, when the Rock of a family dies, this
tells the story of 'wolves in sheep's clothing', a family was split
because the right thing was not done.

My father was real in a vision "to warn" … The beast was real, in animal, and man form.

For whom the child is, God's hand was upon her, for her escape and her long journey to healing, my daughter escaped the beast.

If God is for us, who can be against us.

THE CAROUSEL

Many summers, and many moons
Many lives, come round so soon
Forward on with the circles of life.
Rides low, rides high, the pacing courses
Upon twisty brass and sweet girly names
Those painted mares, the carousel horses.

Here, joy is ours in generations
Fondly we saddle up for fun
Tis these happy days we are together,
Back to our childlike sensations.
To the Great, to the Grand
To the Father, to the Son
Plays the merry old tunes,
On the carousel's beat box band.

The carousel for our family is a generational activity within the fair grounds. It holds for me an emotional joy, that is shared by us all, when we come together. As a poet this tells me from my mind, that down the generations, all that we once were, and all that we are at the moment, circling within the wheels of life going on. Complete with the ups and downs on the merry carousel.

Great-grandmother, grandmother, mother, grandfather, father, son, grandson.

THE CITY GATES

Colonia Nervia Glevensuim is her name
Through time, although it boasts well
Will never lose itself, the Romans claim;
Histories will have it the perfect society
Within the city gates she shall be safe,
The beautiful youth she, in all her beauty
She shall be safe, within military mighty
Yet she resides with the Emperor Nerva,
The highest status her provincial town
Under wing, kingdom of Roman Empire.

Carried great oaks, onward from forest lands
Strong will be the city gates for his empress
Where she will reside in peace from all fates.

But histories have told, The Roman empire fell
Then came invading the breaking of city gates,
Rampage, angered they took her beautiful life
And the heart of the city, the emperors wife,
Cut down by the sword in her beautiful prime
Across the centuries that had passed between,
He came too late to rescue her through time
Lost is Rome, he now weeps at the city gates,
Gallent in bronze on horse for you he still waits.

2014

This historic poem is dedicated to the memory of Hollie Gazzard.

THE COACH THAT NEVER CAME 1959/1979

She knew, she heard, and saw a vision
She had seen, drowned it, closed her ears
This was his fate, it was not her decision
Through the veil, revealed a future fear.
And the coaches, of Tewkesbury's old
When hill steeply whipped up to a tut
The rackety wheels, that galloped hard,
They passed him by, in darkness bleak.

It was that cold and fateful night
In March's snows, where wind did bite
Came at speed, and he ploughed a pole,
With no harness legal, to keep him tight.
Hands to the wheel, that drove the cart
Pressed on deep through his dear heart
And pierced his young spirit, and soul,
Split and spilt both, a brother's blood.

Losing life waiting, whilst he bled
We are slaughtered, whilst you talk,
Play with us, it's just a bloody game
And of old, took an undertaker's son,
Now lies dead, a lifeless twin-less one.
TO THE COACH THAT NEVER CAME.

In memory of my dear cousin, Barry Sweet, written 2011
My vision before he died, I knew that I would lose him soon,
to the powers to be, at that time, and their compassionate care,
with their strikes of 1979.

THE FOLD

At speed we two travel the long road through
Back to the fold hence, came the brotherhood
Greeted, we come to you in the earliest of night
Where the blue mountains burn behind crimson,
And the blue skies afar, were fast losing its light.

The slopes of fields were buttercupped in gold
And the great hawthorns draped like a blizzard,
With the lilacs licking purple those fine counties
All in the glory of Worcestershire's rich bounties.

Dusk entered a harvest moon, loomed above Malverns
Reflecting back the fiery planet that side hidden,
To the mirror of its face, looks into the ages of old
Back to the night my love, we on our two wheels;
On and forever the lonely road in bend and turns;
Old moon gave us its light, we banking the corners,
Without a care in the world, again our lives are told
A love hardly destroyed, "Lost", by God was sealed,
We the future, back we have come; *into the Fold.*

May 2014

First bike meeting on our Yamaha SR 500 after a 35 year gap of
riding ... at Malvern.

THE GIRL FROM APPERLEY

I go back to when we were at school
You showed you cared, if you dared,
For being my friend, but not your best
Although I was, inside your head.
We laughed a lot, a lot we shared
You were dear Glynis, my real friend,
Kept all from Penny, we had to pretend.

When Penny went away on holiday
I came to stay at your house, in Apperley,
The summer's hot and happy days
Walked dearest friends, in country lanes,
Through fields of buttercups, and bales of hay.

At night we watched 70s' TV moody and peg
Raiding the cupboards, not wanting sleep
But promised soon to come to bed.
And when we did, the night was talk
Strange in your house got no sleep at all
Strange country sounds, the dark of night
Slumbered your dad, in a room next door,
His trumpeted sounds of snore, snore, snore.

Twenty-five years later I had a dream
Tall angelic forms, your arms they held
Leading you away, away from me.
Unhappy was your tired small face
As they took you away, away from me,
Cus you had to go on, to another place
But you loved me enough, to come into my sleep,
To say goodbye, goodbye dear friend,
Between dead and living, you are my grief.

Out of my slumbers I still lie here
Where warm and quiet seems my room
My opened eyes, felt a single tear
Dismayed with truth, my impending gloom.
As my hand soon turns, the paper's pages
Again your soft voice tells me to look
Where the deads passing, is in many ages
And there were you, departed from me,
Where in my dream, this became so true.

Written 1990s edited 2012

This is to celebrate the life of Glynis Francis, a dear friend of mine, that never left my heart. Unknown, but known in dreams, she connected with me to depart this life. Real friendship even beyond the wall of life and death. In truth this happened to me, and is still fresh in my mind as ever. Because we had not seen each other for many years, our changing lives and rearing children kept us apart, that death could not.

Her funeral was beautiful, it had shown she was loved dearly, as the church in Apperley was full, my father the undertaker did the arrangements. I remember coming out of the church, and as I stood behind her coffin, I looked down the church path towards a old gate, where a golden wheat field lay ablaze in sunshine, and my mind went back to our school days walking those golden fields in the balmy summer holidays of the 70s … I remember then looking into her dug space and her coffin lowered into it, and soon two single deep red roses was thrown on to her coffin, by her husband and son. Penny was there too with hair to her waist sobbing bitterly, and only I knew of my old school friend's visitation in my dream, my best friend Glynis.

THE GREEN HILL

All that I am, is all that is left open wide
Falls from my head, rests at my feet
For now all of my seasons have seen
In the bluest of skies, there I dreamed.
Company had I, with the centuries of man
At the plough, his labours, and his scythe,
So long ago was my birth in the seasons
When I rose saplinged upon the green land
So long ago kept weary souls in their sleep,
So long ago was found the rubbing of hides.

Upon the green hill where I stood still
Company I, with the centuries of beast
Company I, with the centuries of wings
Sold many a song when the bird sings,
Mornings I, with the breaking of dawns
Ambered warmth at my youth's breast
Gave me turn at going down of the sun
That rests behind the dark rooks' wood,
Speaks blood's goodbye at a day's rest.

Autumn 2014

Upper Load upon the Green Hill. The ancient oaks upon that
fertile land and of other lives.

THE IMMACULATE DEAD

Remembered, immortal through new ages
Set in stone, landmarked and world known,
We relate, to your sense of belonging
Lived the drama, inked within blank pages.
There his words was a heart full of longing,
Where birdsong danced his pure mind,
He once trod her lanes and fields and woods
And peace in her his soul he did find,
From his storms dark, cruel and unkind.

But not for him done, all a poet was said
England's dear fell to France in the spring,
Always his will be now 'England' to keep
Where all birdsong for poetry still sings,
'Wait for us' silent words as you sleep
He is ours 'Edward' The Immaculate Dead.

To Edward Thomas the poet, 2012

THE JOURNEY

There was a still and lingering light
Suspended in time and in frame,
To the wanten coming of the night
Not far from its retiring day.
Her flowering walls, and craggy path
Reaches up into breathless heights
And there for all the world to see
A sky on fire ablaze, orange aflame.

Cast down below, where ebb and flow
Embraces, to the rest of her bosom,
As she waits long for her lover's return
Within Trevaunance's beautiful cove.

Mountains have risen, with men's toils made,
Where the moon beamed whole into the sky
As I turned to see my love sat on the rock
Calling out silent with his mind, to the sea,
We are one you and I, till the close of our lives,
Charles we are one, set in stone, 'Immortality'.

St Agnes. Cornwall, September 2010

THE LION LIES LOW AT LECKHAMPTON

Five long years …
The Lion battles on,
Stands proud his ground
'The Rock' welcome to his game
Rises up, he is forever strong
So be privileged to know him
For what is in a name
Meet with a king,
Share humble, in his domain.

Wandering now the great plains of life
Destined was his, and his alone
Left behind the loves, of child and wife
And the sunny happy, happy home.
Clambers the heights of Leckhampton hill,
While the wailing winds howl overhead
Is waiting there the angels' tender embrace
With love that only angels can fill,
To the living, and the grateful dead.

There, your two loves foraged in the wood
To bring you their last love, and found,
The sweet violet~ clothed in purest white
Pressed firm its scent into your hand,
Where love embraced, and first began.

Amidst the crackle, and dying gasp
I ran to my God in urgent prayer,
With desperate pleas, 'make it not last'
I wrote my God a beggin' letter
'Please take our king', so true, so fair,
To a land of yours, that is truly better.

This poem is dedicated to my father-in-law, Leonard Sidney Ferneyhough, who was a true rock of our family, and a true king of his domain.

He spilled over into people's lives and hearts, and would help anyone, with anything. People who were lucky enough to meet him, and experience his caring thought, for even strangers, had met with a king.

To the caring angels of Leckhampton, and the small boy. Bless your lives and hearts.

Leonard my father in law, died in my arms at Leckhampton March 2008 ~ I give the glory to God for his life, and for making me part of his family.

THE LONG ROAD BACK

Let us take to the high, and low roads
Long and narrow, winding dusty lanes
Up over hills, and to valleys we arrive,
High is the land, through cliff tops' veins.
World's end, 'Sweet Englands' all out to sea
Mirrors the closest sun, flickers and penetrate
Reflects back to heaven, off blues, God's face,
By Bedruthan Steps, breathless, of old.

Then to a rugged, but ragged sign
Crooked but cragged, into the wall
Wavered with winds, points Trevone,
We are adventurous, youth once again
Hand in hand, the echoes back ages call,
Childless a while, together we are alone.

Hot desert grains, roll white dry underfoot
And we lovers plunge deep, within dunes
Whilst we embrace, far coming tides of love
Rushing forth the swells, to her golden plains,
Where rocks are worn, past with many moons
Entices us to her bosom, trickles of other rains
Wide apart, exposed, colours of blackest soot.

And my love sits naked, armoured his flesh
Looking out to sea, upon, in company with
Tight shielded razors, black and sharp;
Black and sharp, as the battles of the mind;
Soon in distance the roar, of the lion's mouth
He has come back to me, now not so far
The white horses wild, break forth a charge
Returns tamed to pools, of dreams left behind,
Rescued anew, born again, sweetly afresh.

Cornwall, Sept 2010

19th September 1981 was when we were married, and our anniversary in 2010 was spent in Cornwall. I wrote this poem from memory a year later in 2011. My poems reflect to me, our relationships with each other, and the journeys that life takes you through. I relate to the world around me, and what I see in it.

THE NEW ESTATE

Like a burning lava, the new estate takes hold
Like infected saliva, comes fast, dribbles over
Their money talks, as the architects walk.
The drafts of the land, 'The New Estate',
With bigger plans, than more will make
Stands now tall and proud, new and bold.
'Human Intervention'

Brick, steel, metals, block, wood
Sand, gravel, concrete, tile, glass,
Her beauty gone, and now replaced
For sickly trees, bush and shrubs
Mirrors the cheap, cultivated face.
'Human Intervention'

Steal, it did, those wheels of steel,
Ripped up, sicked up, rolled inside out,
Dragged up, ragged up, all nature's soul
Invaded her hill, her dale, her field,
Exposing its conception, guts of old,
The centuries real feel, and past yields.
'Human Intervention'

But! then as always, nature shows her face
Yearning, but returning, from concrete land,
As years claim back … supremely gold
In another time, pulls in the human hand
When time forgot, all of the human race,
Came to, came over, came through,
Grew over, took over … 'It's all over'.
'No Human Intervention'

My work as a fixing tiler has taken me to many new builds, upon fair lands. Green belts, and flood plains have been torn to pieces, ruthless, with our machinery. The need for more homes to be built, the explosion of the human race, and of course extra revenues ... This in turn impinges on land that provides for a reason in the control of flooding, and the need that nature has to survive, in these green places, before nature in all forms becomes extinct because of us. Therefore I can say there has been too much land taken away for building houses.

This will in the end be our problem, which has already happened in those very places of being flooded. Nature will always have the upper hand and balance the earth once again, continuing to rebirth ...

As I was having my lunch in the motor one hot June day, I became aware with my environment, upon the New Estate. This was a flood plain, and in 2007 the river came through this estate regardless. In places I could see small meadow field flowers, and emerging grass trying to claim its territory back between block paving ... I felt so true to poet for her cause and thought that, if humans disappeared for some reason, which we will, nature would bury us; up, and over, through, and under, 'Nature always has the upper hand.'

THE NIGHT WILL KEEP

Soon the end of day begins to approach
Behind the hill by the white ancient oaks
Ambered by sunsets blood red aglows
The centuries past time still sets her face,
Upon the hill their place, upon the bones.

Wooded hills afar the rooks fly so black
Into those ambered airs to say goodnight,
Majestic black in hundreds are their order
Swirling forms their places to the woods
Absent from leaf the dark spindled forms,
Against the ambered skies fully occupied.

The silence broken before the day is broke
By appointment flies in time the royal geese,
In arrowed throng their language made song
Across the remnants left of a blooded sky;
And I will live another day with them to sleep,
And I will live another day 'the night will keep'.

2013

From the upper lock to the veteran hill where sunsets grow,
into the fields of gold, and from the hands of people of old, we
worship the sun, God in his finest hours.

OLD COFFIN WORKSHOP 1965~2010

Big old hands, works hard to feed me
Big old hands, lifts his child to the wood
The latched wood, the slatted wood.

Dark is the corridor
Where stacked three rows deep
Peers out shiny new
Like a well-dressed fleet,
And the stairs steep and old
With a rail for your good
Pushes flat back a door,
To a story well told.

Many hand worked benches
Pin ups 50s dart holed wenches,
Big old tools in chests on the floor
Pots of goo, and coffin glues
Bubble thick on the old cream stove.
Button nails, brasses, and soft tasselled braids
Lines a casket so pretty in colour of mauve,
With knobs and handles so expertly made.

Foggy warped windows, drafty roof space
Shavings knee high, all over the place,
Gleeful kicks, flies woody curls about
To a scouring look, and fathers shout,
Gut hell! he says, uncle Roy pees on them,
And it's all on yer bleedin' shoes.

1965 ~ written 2010

The old coffin shop Tewkesbury, that belonged to my family B
Sweet & Sons, Undertakers. was built by my great-grandfather,
Bartholomew Sweet. All coffins were made from beginning to
end by hand. My father Don Sweet took me often to the old
coffin workshop, where I watched him make the coffins.

THE PILGRIMAGE

Holding my hand, as we stride across the wet
The firm sinking drag, laid grains to our feet,
Then climbing, our legs, winced heavy to the top
Both with our brows of a sweet summer sweat
Thudding hearts still as one, pulls us to its beat.

And the pathway worn, is aflutter with many wings
Dancing to its warmth, upon dusty beaten tracks,
And brisk whispers come in, from seafaring winds
Drink in, drink in, my peace, come abide with me;
For the resting mind searches, I hath found thee.

Then whilst upon the warm felt, thermalled levels,
The unperplexed, and fixed, I caught a glance
Ruffled feathers staying steady, ever ready
The shelves of air, He having fine chance,
As a meal was down below, on heathered rocks,
He belonged grown, by the sea in generations,
Of his own kind known, clever to the territory.

Distanced, the bell tower rings upon the hill
Where the grey slates stood up on ends,
Identifies the once living, carves the dead.
We walk together, up the dry path of white
The door opened with a croak of busy years,
Welcomed us in to sweet sickly scents.

There his words jump off the wall into my heart
Piercing me with all, newness and passion,
Rekindling in me the, burning fires of poetry,
Brother of the cloth, you win me over,
With connections, I wish never to part.

I looking out to cloudy light, and mists from sea
Separates us all by the oldest glass,
And the good book to me, with language unknown,
Sits tight with slipping cover, in the dust of years.

And ribbons curl pretty, to the celebrations past
While the pulpit beckons me on to its steps
Now peering beyond, at those vacant chairs
My nature to my thoughts, in question asks,
'Could it be? To set them free, is it me?

I feel the blank stares, and the candles burn on
Ambering upon the walls, the silent wisps
Flickers the still pungent airs, of ancient times,
And up there Jesus limply hangs upon the tree
Into sand and stone, behind the faded paints,
And still there, the coming generations will see,
They, us, those, the church, the saints.

Llyn Peninsula-St Hywyn, 2009

THE PROSPEROUS SEED

Prosperous seed sickly yellow
He's the one given permission
He's the lofty sneering fellow
Will hold you all to ransom
Will hold us all in submission
Cus he ain't going anywhere,
Cus we have gave him extradition …
To send the seed, cus we didn't heed
When we had the need, for speed,
And the multiplied, hungry nations feed.

There he goes all over the lands
Won't stay in his allotted space,
Men the job, it's out of yer hands
Migraining yellows all in yer face
Warm winds blow all over the place,
Rapeseed; the piddly smelling seed,
Like his mate Balsam, he won't hesitate,
To 'OVERTAKE'!

Strangling our native dainty dears
Familiar maidens of those seasons,
Smothers her beauty and fragrances
Ravished and raped for no reasons.
Sneaking up on stream and flood
Grown for the bios, and the oils
Money talks, invading us all,
Of our dear England's native soils.

2012

There is money in the sickly seed, and this summer I have
noticed more fields of stark yellow rapeseed covering the land
of England, in more ways than one. It is most rampant, seeding
itself into all hedgerows, woods, riverbanks, brooks, gardens, on
the motorway verges, and central reservations, anywhere you
wish to look it is there, spilling out of the fields. It smells piddly,
and is unpleasant to look at for long. Also I believe that its pollen
has made hay fever sufferers worse sooner. Sign of the times,
where are the swaying fields of golden wheat? Our native flowers
are going under, and never coming back up for air, because of
rapeseed. The only natural yellow that deserves the name is
buttercups, dandelions, and cowslips, narcissus, celandines and
all native flowers that we know in our green England.

THE ROBIN'S SONG

The robin's song he came here to sing
With his joyous springtime sunny tune,
We watched him build, a family home
And it was here our journeys did begin.
To our broken hearts, in sun and moon
Amidst the bare and dancing willows,
Past autumns leafed, the paths below.

When newest spring still had him here
And true the robin's nest, had come near,
There by his dying bed, with all our howls
Of saddest desperations, and all our fears
Came in his pain, when father had awoke
Then mother cried, when his anger broke,
In a shout that 'it had been fifty years!!'

Now an empty nest, are blooms, exchanged
Silence wails in the garden, vacant for him
Only leaves her now, with summer showers,
The flow of bitter loss, she will cast her tears
That come and go, amidst all pretty flowers,
When the robin comes, to sing for him again.

Soon enough the robin's, little darting shrill
Ending his company with yet another year
Beckons to an empty song, and winter's chill,
Once when life, the robin's babes came near
And faded fast, when father's absence brings,
Winter's empty songs, when the robin sings.

2008

113

This is the story of a delicate family time, when my father-in law was put to bed, in his illness in March 2008. I remember him sitting on the bed, and saying to me as I sat by him, and he himself knowing that he was home to die, sat upon the bed fully clothed, trying to look brave to his coming defeat, and said to me 'How's my babby then' ... I gave him the blank stare of 'what me', as he waited for my answer, and I stupidly said and have regretted it ever since, do you mean Charlie or Maryanne? He bowed his head, and shook his head, as if to say 'don't you know by now you are my babby ...' Even though I was his daughter-in-law, I felt that his blood children were his babbies, and he was disappointed that I did not recognise that ... my place in his heart. When you are stressed to the max at such a tragedy, and you are waiting for the person to fade away before your very eyes, and you love that person so much as I did, my whole faith drained from me. Being a Christian, family looked to me for an answer, and I felt so responsible, but this was not what God expected of me, it was his and his alone. I was angry and destroyed, for some time after my father-in-law's death, and it took time for me to turn my faith back around, and to be easy with myself.

THE SONS OF ENGLAND

I stand and look to those early morning dews
As the sun rises across the lonely hill of hearts
Sparkles on each son, wavering blades of grass,
Whilst hard the grey seas of glass, crashes wild
Beyond from the marooned ancients rock aghast;

Then

My eyes are cast above to blue skies in early morn
Where free skylarks dance and sing in their flight,
I am reminded of you all, where you rose and fell
Freedom from those wings instead of guns to fight
Was a dream they had hoped for, only to envisage
Waiting for over the top soon into the mouth of hell,
The whistle blows for our sons to take on a charge.

True the blood of England's sons when for us flows
The alternate price was paid, in all of their sacrifice
For us all in the son of Christ; as only Jesus knows.

October 7th 2013, 9.27 am, upon the field at the coast of Trevone.
Dedicated to the sons of England.

The theme to this poem 'The Sons of England' came to me
upon the cliff top field from Trevone Cornwall. The rich young
grasses were fresh and green in their prime as the clear night
before had cast its heavy dews upon each grass blade. The
early morning airs from the wild seas down below came across
drifting its chill to the grasses tightly knit together, making each
blade of grass bend, to and fro, in motion to the same bowing
movements. Skylarks danced about the new blue morning all in

joyous chorus singing on the wing, as the warm low sun behind me, just coming up over the hill reflected pure new sunlight to each dewy blade of grass, and upon that note it came to me that each one of these grasses were a son, each with souls of a millions tears reflecting like diamonds, one from each soldier lost in mind and body. The grey seas of glass crashing beyond them was their war.

THE TOR

I was in slumber and remembered
The old rugged Cornwall landscape,
Made men with toils of heaving sweat
Worked hotter in bitter cold not kind
Those Cornish winds cursed and wet;
Came the grey giants new in the land
Are now grey ghosts of ruins left behind
Enshrined Cornwall harsh and ambered.

Barren land worked tired and deserted
Grasses tufty on boggy dips and mound,
Under vaulted rock glinted granite black
Hammered carved out the minered ground
When men young made, broke old backs,
Days end stands ruined with the test of time
Grounded towered windowless grey churches.

September 2009 I came to Cornwall and stayed at Charlestown, we visited my sister Maryanne who lives at Minions, Bodmin Moor. At that time we visited the Tor which was a long walk up to this strange monument. The path in the earth to it had been worn by many people coming here like sheep tracks. The impressions left from the 19th century mining working past wheel houses stand enshrined like vacant churches. The land is rough but beautiful with its barrenness. Maryanne has said that there is still ground that gives up its firm surface, caving in from the worked mines. She told me a story about a dog called Cracker that fell down one of these mines, that can be very deep. It was a job to get this poor dog out, and it stuck in my mind because she did not know if they were successful. I have heard of sheep farmers losing their flock down these holes that just cave in, from the minered ground underneath. Closer to where my sister Maryanne lives on the moor in a field at the back of her garden, she was told of a whole tractor that was left by the owners when work was over, only to return the next day to find the tractor had gone down into an old mine swallowed up for all time.

THE TOUCH

The mists of the Wye, and veils adrift moves
Rising to the skies, with early morning dews,
And the coming lights, of a dawning sun
Kisses the white swathes that had begun
Of ambered shades, and warm shafts anew,
Born into the cool starts of another day.

But soon into this wake of the fresh hour
Bowing heads moist, holds up their praises
Once again, to the great God fire on high
Multitudes, releases, into haze and beam,
Their existence, and persistence, to redeem.

Balsam keeps a hold on us all, into submission
Their temptatious aromas, 'heady' its beauty,
Ahh! fragrant, fertile, sweet and fruity
Born obsessed, possessed, determined,
On going, on going, asks no permission.

Throughout her woods, they have imprisoned
Regimented in numbers, they do not belong,
Rooting out, veins through, ruthless cruel
The marsh and wood, no natives can hide,
Explodes the seeds of battle, these warriors
They are carried easy, rampant upon the tide.

March on, march on, see their great parading
To the hum of bee wings, and gentle bird songs,
Those purpled giants, in confident throngs
Beating an alien heart, through land invading.

And nature tells us, upon every season
Her occupants have their rightful place,
'God then put man's hand to the scythe' when,
He cuts them down and made fast to chase
Against the clock, he throws his poison.

It could be too late, when man in his haste
Tries to save our natives, that God created
For now she is the balsam woods ... and has,
Rooted over, strangled tight, dark and dingy,
The woods gave up her rights, now ill fated
And in her gloom, gave up on her waiting.

The rampant weed Balsam, that is a invader of our shores, pretty as it looks, it is strangling our native woodland beauties to extinction. It is 'the balsam' that is not controlled regularly enough, and to be controlled. At Redbrook in particular, I caught sight of balsam marching high up into the woods, from river bank to fields and woods. It is a poet's word to warn. 2010

THE WAITING ROOM

Father's on his way, in mind he did said so
I felt him look to me, within trees so dark,
Amidst family laughter by the gate and path
I felt his pains, within his, and my own heart,
Daddy so strong, please daddy don't go.

Our smiles between, our blue eyes last met
At your back door, happy I was more, but a;
Goodbye to father, goodbye to daughter,
I left you daddy, with a strange white aura?.

"Should I be surprised?"

Whilst into the coming of the night
Was when I kissed and last left you,
I looked to the dull skies, for din and cries
Where daddy flew away with a flock of geese,
Purest of breed, he the angelic seed.

Then another day next at noon, you died;
So heavy I walked, I walked back to you
And with every step, and every breath, me ...
I was the walk, the walking, living dead.
I climbed a thousand stairs up to your bed;
There you laid, nothing said, "my angelic one"
Your pains had gone, and mine had begun.

True ... I thanked God for having you
But wanting more for keeps, more of you,
Blue, your eyes looked up to heaven, so so blue.
Angelic one of mine, you belonged to me;
I prayed please to let him in, "God said yes"
As warm went cold, I knew that you had left.

Then mother's steps creaked up the stairs,
Stood at the door way, weak with despair
She looked through me hollow, with disbelief,
Then laid close by father, gazed to his still face
So silent, no tears, just ... silence,
Looking, wanting, and waiting, as if to wake,
But alone now beats her aching heart
The wall inside her, silent, the wailing grief.

And children played near, all their young days
When father went on to church
Living the church, all the days of his life,
Upon other people's sorrows and strife
And now he gets to ride in his own hearse.

Time does pass, I count the hours awake
Time does pass I count the days by,
Time does pass I count the weeks
Further away from me father, bitter I cry,
Pleading my God, that I needed to seek
Please let me see, let me see, if he's safe.

Then one night, such a dream came to me;
It was father, sat on a small stool, in the kitchen
With his head in his hands, surrounded by bitching,
I looked on as he pleaded, the cause to his plans
He thought he had done right, "can't they see"?

Father came forward, he came forward, to me
With his eyes full of tears, so blue, so blue
When silence moved to his lips, ... I understood
That his burdens, I will soon bear, and should,
Stay strong but free, and would, very soon
See father waiting in ... "The Waiting Room".

This is a true poem of the coming strife, and the answer I received from God, in the week my father died. The dream given to me was more than I expected, and these events in my life not long after the dream came true with speed. "I have never been so hurt". But the only comfort to my dream was that God told me in pictures, my father was safe and waiting. No voices or language were heard by me, because God can make you understand in silences. The continuing dream came to an end, where I followed behind father. In procession behind me were my mother and siblings, when we came to the great doors, which looked like barn doors, my father opened these doors with both hands, and stepped inside of the doors, to face me. He held the doors, so I could not enter with him. I stood on my toes to peek over his shoulder, to see what was the other side. It was a warm amber room, with soft lights on the walls. I looked back at father, and he gave me that look like, you cannot enter it is not your time, but I am waiting. He then closed the doors slowly, and I awoke to another day. "God gave me my answer."

THE WHITE HOUSE

The white house dominant
A vacant house with many rooms,
Stands at the foot of Doward's Hill
Laned from rat race's stifling fumes,
There vacant people and vacant light
Falls to the woods, becomes entombed
No twinkles here upon the fall of night.

There along the Doward lane
Where giant chestnuts grow,
Is the long road home, and still,
I see the white house strange
Stood at the foot of Doward's Hill,
For miles out of landscape range
A beacon house in daylight glows.

The white house is the place I know
A place I wish, I wished I owned,
Its presence there, in my memory
Can only look, but will always see
The white house far away, and still,
Stood at the foot of Doward's Hill.

2012, The Danter family

THOSE LITTLE EYES

Up into the Mythe above the tut
Warm spring winds they did so blow
Amidst great oaks where chestnuts grow,
Where the multitudes are in many decades
Nested thick with black squarking crows,
And hidden in holly just underneath,
A fluffy coned nest fell out in a heap.

Upon a hot unforgiving path down below
The cradle was full and rolled about,
As crows up above cawled an easy meal
Mother was gone, but this mother did say,
"We must rescue our four feathered friends
As it will be our efforts to save their day".

Huddled with silence, two had fell out
With our chasing the nest as it tumbled,
And two did I catch, a bird in each hand
Warmth in my grasp I felt so humbled.
They looked to me with mercy in eyes
As if in ill fate cud ask for a pardon,
No food for you, and what could we do?
Wrapping all into my daughter's cardigan.

To the vale in Beckford and new is the spring
Is where in cage and tree the birdies sing,
And human mothers gather the bird broods
Snug, safe and fed, huddle in hatted feathers
Comforts knowing no difference in species,
Gained human mothers; all growing together.

This story is about a spring day in May, it was most blustery and the blossoms of all were at the mercy of these strong winds, as were most bird nests they were also into the tall towering trees. My daughter Jezica had finished work at the coach house, and was walking home when tumbling down the path in front of her was this little nest, all fluffy and weaved into a cone shape, with four little goldfinches tipped out. Jezica phoned me and we came to these little birds' plight. The crows up above in the tall oaks and chestnuts cawed so noisy into the winds attending to their own with talk about each other, possibly not knowing a possible meal was down on the path below for their own babes. The parents were absent from the little finches and did not return for some time. Nevertheless the nest could not be put back. As we tried to stop the nest being blown out into the fast road, two babes fell out, so I picked them up, having one in each hand. I could feel the warmth of their weak bodies in my palms, and as I spoke to them their little eyes looked to mine in mercy, and remained still knowing I was not mummy. We wrapped them in Jezica's cardigan and drove them nest and all to The Wildlife Centre in the Vale of Beckford, where human mothers look after, and nurse baby birds and injured animals. Our goldfinches were put into a hat lined with familiar feathered nest material, and with two other goldfinches found a few days before somewhere else. It is said that these little birds need feeding every fifteen minutes, then they let them free when strong to fend for themselves. So our little birds from Tewkesbury will live in the Vale of Beckford at peace in a village community, choosing a much safer place to nest their own babies.

THROUGH ROCK & WITHY

Soon the darkness looms "Yat Rock" and black depths
Awakens our tranquil thoughts to the great curve,
When we handle the speeds of flowing through
Mermaid's hair adorned with all her daisies true,
Bursts of white and yellow into summer's lazy hours.

And we two in company with the busy lamprey
Into the shallow waters of the River Wye,
There the damsels court amidst the pink stalked lilies
Whilst our paddles drips rings like a opening eye,
Upon the millponds surface of better days.

Here the old white cottage tumbles back into the woods
Loved but lonesome in company with Rock and Withy,
One day I say ... we will live there in our dreams
Within woods, neighboured, peregrine, buzzard, birdsongs,
Then from his slumber the stag deer rises to look at me.

Upon my calm waters I say to him "I will paint you"
When years later I kept my promise, I still see,
Many times I closed my eyes, and there you are
Forever in mind and paint "we are as one true"
Canvassed there you are 2014 ~ in summer's 2003.

2014

There is a painting connected to this poem from the summer of
2003. We passed this cottage by canoe on the river Wye in the
twelve years with and without children, and not a soul was ever
seen there. It was as if nature neatly managed its own courses
in the cottage becoming engulfed by the withy banks and woods
above it and each side of it. Black and grey mattered rock with
the seedlings of beeches upon its shelves, commanded a fort
cradling the cottage within itself.

WHEN YOU LEFT

Fact

You would go anywhere to take away the sting
Out of; thrown in, you drift in this empty space,
Inside your heartaches, no more room to sing
The black void and empty place, black blind,
Your mind, cannot see his absent happy face.

My Thoughts

His warm hand has left, yours hanging empty,
Nature's course, snatched your love of plenty
To us, you look and remember your own kind
Yet look further from us and see, the others;
You made together, we came from you both;
Love who walks with you and still; just behind
How will you go on? You're not looking so strong.

Mind body and spirit where is finding the will?
Over is your time of love, but to come in nurture.
What is left with love now? What is this future?
It's done, set in stone, heart and mind everlasting.

Mary

I will go on for our kind showing them how to find,
Some sure peace and purpose in my meanings
Fighting from this grey place, and yet gleaning
All the fruits of happiness was found and ours,
Of all those seconds, minutes and happy hours
Days, months, years, and many a decade ...
But, my fears, my tears, bursts in gentle showers
Within all the pretty flowers, my mind have faded
Without you my love the woods colours are jaded,
Yet in my pain for you I try to learn to live again
Beginning to share in their lives, love and cares,
Of our people he left from himself, amidst my pains.

2008

The scene is set in the woods by the river Wye by Yat Rock, and
the year is autumn 2008. Here I see Mary my mother-in-law,
walking besides us deep in her thoughts and at a loose end, a
void I tried to fill for her, but it was not mine to try. At the time
I did see her pain, but mine was so real as well to support her
and my husband. We all went for a walk along the river path as a
broken family, someone, this person, our rock, was missing from
us, and in these times of his absence the future looked bleak.
Our first born grandson Callum was two years old at the time,
and he came with us all, along the river path. In my mind I felt
his presence gave Mary veiled insight into the extension from

which herself and dad had given, in Callum and maybe other great grandchildren to come later. It was emotionally draining to write this poem of pain, but it is what I felt in Mary at that time, and it is her in my mind, her speaking in her thoughts and feelings, as I watched her in her pain of loss, which applies to all of us, as the other is left to live without our spouse.

Nature has to take its course in birth and death, and nature constantly tries to comfort us with the fact that we have succeeded to go forth and multiply and, for most, the gift of new lives in generations from us has to be a comfort ...

YOU CHOSE ME

If the Lord permits me not to stay
Cry not for me another day
For you it will be God's good will
To be glad of knowing me, and still;
See me within all springtime flowers
In forest glades cool summer showers.

I am in the waters of the gentle Wye
That twinkles softly as it runs by,
I am on the souring buzzard's fawny wings,
As she glides upon those dizzy heights
And I am in the screecher's lonely call
Within the trees on dark forest nights.

I break the dawn by name and birth
I keep Christ's month; the planet earth,
I am the new morn the lord God brings
A voice of many, when blackbird sings
Of Jesus' heart, and for all he's worth.

I'm in woodland courses of those streams
And the swaying trees in blousy breeze,
I'm all of Wales, she's all of me,
In life on earth, and in all my dreams
I will take her with me to eternity,
But look for me you will find me there
In true Wales so blue, my land so fair.

May 2013

"She Choose Thee"

This poem was written at Whitebrook, a month after falling ill with heart failure, just after my book Forest Diaries had been published and available on 15th April.

I did not know what my survival rate would have been, and I felt that all I had planned before this illness after my book launch, had been lost. I felt the need to leave this poem behind, drawing on my memories in case the worst should happen.

YOUTH IN MAY

In May born, the may, my old friend hawthorn
Becomes adrift with blizzards, of tumbling snows,
And beyond shines lush fields of buttercups gold
Take my hand, walk with me, where I often go,
I am still a child, but then, I am not quite old.

And upon the hill, old oak still drops his swing
Where once our childhood memories were bright,
Of young laughter and fun, it did us bring
Upon your old arm safely hanging there,
Without care, reaching those cloudy heights
Maytime and birdsong, chatters all around
With its din a throng, to the sweet airs of spring.

The willows fresh, reside many at river's edge
Casts her fluffy seeds to the gentle breezes,
And holds out her wisps, for you to touch
Temptations to feel her soft virgin teases
When released away from clammy fingers,
Grateful for your visit, thank you very much.

Walking river's path, waist high in hemlock
The sun's departure low, gave an orange fire glow,
Across the ploughed fields, the haze's frenzy yields
Above within still air, their dances of all flitty flies.
Woods had perfectly hid, his early song the cuckoo
And misty into distances, trills through airless airs,
Calls for love the sweet and graceful curlew.

2012
Tewkesbury lock, onward to Lowerlode Forthampton.

GENERATIONS

In the late summer, September beckoned
Autumn's twist of another season
Amidst, the long dry leafy lane.
An avenue of horse chestnuts each side met,
Together at their tops like clasped hands.

The still warm breezes came through
A coppice of trees, leaves now few,
From the harvested fields yonder
The secluded tunnel of chestnuts
All in a frenzy tossing their bounty,
Ripe and loosed …
From great ageless heights
Casting the year's bud and fruit,
Their seed soul and kind,
To the hard track lane below
And neighbouring verge, and fields,
In hopeful reproduction cast their years.

Split prickly cases hit hard the old way
Revealing the prizes of silk, and bronzed fruit,
Still moist from its soft womb,
With the scents of its mother's earth.
She shall not be baron in many generations
She shall produce in her life's generations,
In ours, and in future generations.

In the lane at NIA … Twigworth Gloucester 29.9.15

PITCHCOMBE

I hear the soft cooing of the dove
In the bosom of Pitchcombe valley,
Amidst the small sway of the breezes
Wooded on every side,
Laid bare the sloped meadows
Rich and fertile, under the sky,
Where the beasts now resides
In life, and in all of its forms.

Hear now the rustling of the beech leaves
Into each and with turn,
The gentle late summer rains
Full dewy the humid airs warm
And with all love's troubles and concern,
Finds peace in the heart and soul
Soothing the mind, like poets glad,
Here is the home, "The Slad."

August 2016

A poem about the Slad valley, me, and Laurie Lee, and where
home is, in the mind of a poet.

YOUR MEMORIAL

Your memorial, at the foot of the Malverns
In the month of June,
Not quiet the decade
At summer's height, mid-afternoon.

You and your new motorbike, I heard often,
Now silent to the blue mountains
They have claimed you, now set in stone,
Homeward bound, you were our own.

Bright now in this autumn blaze
And misty Sunday morning haze,
The church fine in its glory
And the smallness of your dying place,
A corner from those dark woods
In other flowers you rest your face.

You one of us, we survived long ago
My biker friend, it is sadness for us to know
Where you are now and your smooth roads
Away from all of humanity and fools, and yet,
Hopeful are we of more, you lead the way,
As you were there before.

Thumper Hill, joyous to be back for me from death's door
Is where my life unfolds, back to youth,
And laughing, but now finally old
It could never be an unhappy road.

Hollybush, your memorial is more than we can take
And many ride and will your way in other seasons,
For all their joyous and dedicated reasons
The hilly, winding and the straight.

Dedicated to a fellow motorcyclist
who was killed in June 2019 at Hollybush Malvern.

DORIS

I was born of Christmas, within my grandmother's arms
At winter's breaking dawn and blizzard snows,
Helpless to the world; walking and running, I know not of,
And hunger, I do not yet understand.

I am within the elements, I am the earth of earth …
I stare up at the skies, up out of her strong embrace,
Where meeting from my infant trances
We look into each other's eyes.
And I knew with my infant mind, "Instinctual"
That I came from you …

26.12.15. The Old Boathouse Lyme Regis

My birthday, my grandmother Doris Sweet.

THE OCEAN'S EYE

I came forth from the land
And walked boldly across its plains
Given legs, I was human.
But I remember when I was born to you,
And crawled out away from your hand,
The worst betrayal of kinship from man.

I am now tired of this existence
Reclaim me back from the dead,
Home is easy, where there is no resistance.

The underworld of my planet dark
Beamed light into my beginnings,
From the bed of that care made.
I looked up as grains of sand, my deep waters,
Temptations … it just would not fade.

I lived and died and morphed
Into the capable breed,
From creature, to mammal
To animal, to man, his image God's seed.

Through ages, I betrayed you from my births,
Beginning to breathe airs through nostrils of
Animals and man.
Given two legs, I was drawn away
With the intelligence to understand,
The Garden of Eden, the form of a higher race,
We both became of man.
He was she, and she was he
And betrayed him too,
Where all beauty was within that sinless place.

Bedruthen Cornwall 2014

A poem about the beginnings of time, and man's sin against God. The relationship to get back to a relationship with him, and the human condition.

YOUTH OF A GIRL

The youth of a girl, the young Christian
Brought up, and into, the presence of God.
Her hope, and the innocence of it,
She looks lovingly into peace
And the contentment of it.

There is Jesus in her every step
Knowing nothing yet, of suffering to come,
But foundations are laid in her heart,
And the seed hath been sown.

And there I envied for a moment
How once my foundations were not moved,
And longed to be that innocent again.

2019 Malvern, written at the Christian cafe
A poem about lost faith in life.

MY MIND IN LAMPLIGHT

Here I am by my lamplight
And memories of you come to my mind
In poets ET ... good book, and I must write,
That vision in my mind's eye
In bluebelled forest, the Doward Woods.

Sat all alone upon an old tree stump
With heavy heart, I knew nothing of,
And you with full eyes
The saddest look, into the hues,
Of springtime magic, the bells of blues.

Slowly you catch sight of me
From distance looking up at you,
I see in all your hollowness and grief
The future set to no relief, and yet,
We are still here with no regrets.

My book, our love, but first my death
Is looming close, a miracle it would not be
My time away from other snows, and yet,
My poetry did not die with me ...

Better times after I have come back to this place
Seen many springtimes, summers upon sister rock,
With forest views and woodland landscape.
No peregrine here or piercing calls,
Only serene the buzzard's crafted flights and fall,
To dusky woods when the sun escapes.

And there I speak again to the screech and hoot
The owls my fondest feathered friends,
Where I with them take a walk,
Into the night and there, within those blousy trees
We communicate and once again talk.

Dedicated to my husband Charlie, in Doward Woods, 2012

THE VISIT

I have come back to the old familiar place I know
In hazel wood, where, the ancient trees did grow,
Dark twisted, gnarled and ageless
Lichened, mossed in majestic greatness
Foundations found in the drover's road
So many stories lost, they have seen and told,
To me in poetry.

I hear you and walk your way, in company
With your elder, the giant chestnut,
And your descendants, the rugged oak
The twisted chestnuts, and tall silver beeches
With the stretched, carved in time, timeless,
Lovers' names ...

I return in another year, of years past
When the good book was done ... a wet spring,
And there you are, slain and lain
No more the canopy of the darkest woods,
And only light now guides my way
In this humid sabbath noon,
Where you were once saplings
Along the craggy drover's road,
Cut down with all your stories and seasons
Back to the earth, too soon.

With my grief, I hurry off away to investigate
The further culling of your elder's fate,
With anxious heart, and quick step
Slipping around underfoot, about the forest floor,
The soils waterlogged, as you drink no more
To make my way easy,
All now left, is a sprawling, pooling bog.

The heat of the season, late spring is rising
The sting of the midges are fiercely biting,
My breath they seek, and my coursing blood
Where yours from this land has ceased.
I walk upon it, and your life force is buried
Where I come to my destination, with relief,
Here your ancestor and descendants still grow
Into the earth of this fair land
Still grounded from birth, majestic and grand ...

But the multitude of foxglove and purple hues
Within your airy shadows, willowy they grew,
Forced their way for the sun and the light
In your company, with their allotted season
Are now no more, taken, a colourless life.
Strangled by weed and unruly ferns
Undertook, overtook, and over turned,
Captive they lain buried, in red rooted earths.

Hazel wood 2013/2019
By Wulstans Farm, Gloucestershire/Herefordshire borders

THE ASYLUM

Set in the county of Gloucester
Within the landscape of ambered skies
Bestowed upon its form.
Those broad ambered skies at the end of a day
Giving simple refuges with the thought in mind
Of its architectures, and calming effects,
A natural world from all its madnesses
Within a day lived a human soul locked in.

I see my mother, at mother's house where both are lost.
There I see her sat in her ivory tower, my mother ...
The winding staircase that she has climbed up to the top
With her feet as heavy as the leaded roof,
Of her pinnacle into that mindless room.
There she sits encased within her time capsule
With the steel door shut tightly behind her.

There is one small window looking out
        to the horizons of life outside
The window just small enough
        to be level with the chair she sits on,
As she waits for the coming of the sun
        to light up her mind, but,
The sane reality and refuge she longs for
        is all that is left in her empty world.
Each day she has to climb to the top
        from the bowels of this stark reality,
That his end has come, and he no more can carry her through.
This journey is well travelled every day just to exist,
In the reality of absence and loss, and alone.

She has shut me out, she will not let me in
She is out of my reach unreachable by far this woman …
It was a long time ago I was in the womb
She has let me go my own way never to return …
There is mother, there is where she sits in the chair,
Waiting for the sun to go down, as it disappears so does he,
The love of her life, casting darkness once again all lost.

The sun rises, and she climbs the stairs once again
He will be there, to the top, she arrives to the room,
Where reality does not visit for a time yet, no pain.
She waits ambered like blood, he will arrive very soon
Into her sanity and refuge if just for a while.
There she will sit and then the peace floods her existence,
Once again resting those demons of insanity.

2013
The insanity of loss, the journey it takes you to, and the strength of time.
Location of Coney Hill Asylum.

THE COUNTIES

We climb high to the top of the hills
From counties below, of our birth you and I,
From our youth, it is time
On the eighties smooth classic,
Is where we both ride.

And yet, I unknowingly
Just a girl, my future was prepared,
He, asked for my hand in marriage,
Father weary to commit
His first born child to the lair.

The daily paper lifted up to father's face
Awkward, mother takes the place,
of … "That will be nice"
Waiting, but silence, I was told.

Continued …

Destination at the top from counties down below
In this youth, we come together
Like birds of a feather,
Where the drama is in a theatre road.
I look up over his shoulder, to the sheep
Grazing in white numbers upon the hill,
He asks for my hand, five years past
At last, he will be mine for keeps.

Thirty six years later rings are lost
Hearts had crossed, and at a cost.
He once again, in all my pain
Bought me that ring at theatre road,
Where we are not young, but had gotten old,
And came to visit once again
From fair counties down below.

There was a time away from youth
Where we both had proof
Of our bubbles broke,
And where I had left my heart
Upon those hills, with love that filled
Not theirs, but ours,
That others could not kill.

Malvern 1979/80
Malvern 2016
Written December 2019

THE BREAK OF DAWN

I stand at my window naked into the winter warmth
Distant of the sun, I am now born, out of Christmas,
At the break of dawn … and if I were able to go to the sea,
There I would find you, waiting for me.

I stand alone upon the rocks, then close my eyes,
I fall into your arms, the embrace of deepest swell of ebb
      and flow,
Swirling and consumed under the great wave of your love.

Sometimes you will toss me back, out upon those rocks,
And you will dash me hard, and you will cut me to pieces
      "my heart";
And I cannot get a grip to my rock that I once stood so
      firmly upon.

Not even barnacles rest my plight,
But to cut my bloodied feet, "helpless, just helpless,"
Unrescued, your wrath spits at me with force,
      the pounded wave,
Oh! how it stings my skin, cold and sharp like the
      "Sting of Death",
Crushing my heart, taking my breath, leaving me hollow
      with no soul
Colder is your love, than the rotting grave.

26.12.15. The Old Boathouse Lyme Regis
About life and foolish gain and loss

THE YEARNING

As I watch the sea from my window
I think of our love, strong as storms in our hearts,
The white horses rage on towards me,
Rage on, rage on, with your helpless destructive song.

Gallop towards the battle, come to me, you the knight of
    my life
Majestic, you, that white horse.

No calm of ebb and flow, I wait on the shores, as you try
    to reach me,
"Back and Forth" I wait, I wait, with brokenness,
And absence to take your hand, so out of reach, but I can,
See you there always in the angry sea.

"Fear not" you have taken me to where I belong with you
Under the sea within our dreams,
It is where we belong, you and I, in this love ...
And there we hide under the waves as the storm rages on
Rages on, overhead, back to the shores of my heart.

22.12.15. Lyme Regis The Old Boathouse
Life changes of love

FERTILE EARTH

I will write another story about, the same story
The same place in time, that was my body's end,
Within that landscape, upon heights of Coppet Hill,
The fresh fertile morning, and my womanhood.

My youth's lifeblood dwindling away from me
And the new chapter of my life,
Coming out into another landscape
Of other creatures in their new strife,
Where mine had gone forever
To be able to produce my own kind again.

I had reproduced in my latter times
In all the landscape of the forest,
Down by the river Wye.
Yet my youth had reproduced in words
And in doing upon the landscape,
In rock and river, immortalised forever
In word and child, with mommy's cries,
Fields of gold, daisy chains and clover pink,
Laughter and a mother's smiles,
We are all of her, "Set in Stone".

To my children ~ Coppet Hill 2009

152

BIRTHRIGHT

I am here in that familiar place
As not so long ago, watching, watching,
In lost loves' thoughts ∼
Where the strong hold of the ocean's embrace.

You came to me like a flood, through my blood
As my lover, ruthless you came, set me on fire,
Teasing me, taunting me, with your desires,
Licking about my stable feet, enticing my being
I fall deeply into your jaded waters evermore
And I do, I do let you take me, my soul, it is yours.

A poem about the gladness of life
At Bedruthen Cornwall in 2014.
The ocean gave me my future,
I was not lost after all.

FATHER AND ME BY THE SEA

From the holed hill looking out to sea
There we are, just daddy and me,
The long path and the lush fields across
Full with the ocean's kissed spring greens.

The way we cycle is hedgerows and cliffs
And the expanse of the sea down below,
In my mind's eye it is a Sunday afternoon
Comforted, I am only three years old.
Sitting on my own little seat of red tartan
On the front of my father's bicycle.

The summer of 1962 is hot
And the old road is bumpy and dusty,
We glide past those full hedgerows
Daddy says hold on to the bars,
All I want to do is hold on to daddy's arm,
That strong hairy arm, I am now safe.

Up against my father and the scent of his arms
And the love I felt for him
Love was familiar, love was safe
How else would a child know love for a father.

This memory has been with me all my life
And here I am at sixty, on the path at Trevone
Although my distant memory tells me so,
It is the old station yard back home,
When trains were still big old chuffers.

I am now with father on this a Sunday
Riding with father on his bicycle
Upon this warm dusty path by the sea.
I feel the warmth of his body
I smell the scent of his arms
I feel the love of my father,
And I will imagine him anywhere,
That fits in my memory ...

Trevone Cornwall 22nd September 2019

POETS SPEAK

My favourite poets …
Edward Thomas, and Ivor Gurney
I cannot chose between the two,
And yet my poet friend and sister
With her play The China Bowl,
And her poems more than many
Is my dearest, Charlotte Mew.

The walking Poet of Dymock,
Or the musical poet of Severn,
Or the gentle poet of London,
All are native in their craft
Their words in my mind's eye
Are the gems in times gone past.

Their words are all I have to cling to,
Those words etched in my mind
Are all of that is magic, in all of earth I find.

_2019_

TREVONE

Fallen away from its birth made and prehistoric forms
Swathed in the ocean that covered the new earth
Birthed a volcanic once born, to age with time
A future in ocean, I know nothing of,
But God did, he knew me well.
My ancestors were sand, and lived there until
Form was taken within my pen.

The gorged rocks reveal their inner cores
From the pounding forces, and the beat,
Elemented and moulded with heat
And Ice, melting the heart of God,
As he played with you in his hands.

Those Rocks, black as the night
With florescent mid split cores,
Laid and pressed white.
Marble, a sharp stark statement made
Cave like, cubby, cosy, "Occupied".
Upwards, across, over, under, roofed, holed,
Carved, shaped, smoothed, by the carpenter's hand
Knowingly under the right volume of waters.

Reveal your soul waiting upon every tide
To meet and depart forever more,
Until you are pummelled and grinded back to glass
Now in company with the black razors
Back to the grind of time from beginning to end.

Dialogue

The black razors, armoured, protected
Regimented, soldiered, shields of war
Only taking places, within their allotted spaces,
Time is short for their generations.
But when they become weak and lose grip on life
Against the great ocean's force, they fall pearly sided
Open to the grind of ebb and flow soon to be,
Refined back to sparkled sands that adorn the sea,
And the garden's grave of rest.

I unknowingly took with me this dark place
Within its beauty and innocence
When the lies were over and denials of life,
I was in the wars of love and madness,
Losing my grip on living, being replaced.

Just sweep me away with your tide
Bury me back to the **"Oceans Eye"**,
Where I first came from, God nurtured me there
In the safety of his hand, before I walked the earth.

Trevone Cornwall in 2016, Edited on September 19th 2019.

The birth of the landscape,
and how we will all disappear back to who made us.

WITHIN THE STORM

Rushing in to meet me, oh what a journey you have.
The sun is on your back and the wind is on your tail
Hindering your flow, and your destination to my heart,
Struggling against my struggles, you weaken and fade
Unreachable, untouchable, is our forbidden my love.

But like the gravitational pull upon the earth it will be,
"Set in stone, for all time, even as the earth consumes us,
We lived in her time and felt, and loved in her time
This time, our time, time on forever.

The stars explode and we are as earth, will be matter
Into the equation of a trillion stars
Labelled with all of humanity's scars
And all that God maketh at his command
He taketh our paths ...

22.12.15. The Old Boathouse Lyme Regis
About life changes of love and loss

UNDER THE SKY

Amidst all suns, all rains, all snows, all mists
Days and nights, starry skies and moons
The crevice river, between rocks, under water,
The sea ... Laurasia;
Now carved its space in my lifetime.
I watch its course, low between, and under the sky
Out of the sea, you are mighty, but a brook.

I travelled on you in my craft, through
Your courses plenty, from mighty mountains Wales,
Pure, cleansed and mineralled, out on to the sea ...

Your woods, covered the sea beds
Where wolf roamed, and bear wandered,
The deer gentle in your spaces.
And man hunted for food and clothes
Lived in caves with animal ancestors,
And their own dead ...

The drover travelled many miles through
From wood to wood and stayed ...
But now in my time ...
Fossil fuels have got me here
And I hear the machines, that cut,
Those woods of peace,
Tranquillity and living
For man and beast.

Great Doward, April 2019

LOVE BY THE SEA

Love is,
Being driven to the top from the cob by the sea
After high tide and a rough autumn night
He drives me, up into the early morning light.
From my slumber, and I rocking blissfully lie,
Watching the sky, and treetops up the hill go by,
There we stop, just at the top, where the robin sings
And the morning fresh airs against my skin stings.

He, and we, just you and me
Listening to Sunday lovesongs, on the radio,
And making on uncle Jim's old stove, cups of tea.
Tomatoes in a saucepan bubble away ready
And we eating a stick of bread and butter
A start to a new day, in memories and renewed love.
This is love, love between you Charlie and me.

Listening to love songs, and drinking tea
Eating tomatoes with a stick of bread and butter,
*Still in bed and, ~ **Love by the sea** ~*

November 2019 Lyme Regis

INDEX OF FIRST LINES